Haunted Berkshire

Haunted Berkshire

Angus Macnaghten

Countryside Books
NEWBURY, BERKSHIRE

First published 1986

COUNTRYSIDE BOOKS
3 Catherine Road
Newbury, Berkshire

ISBN 0 905392 58 2

Produced through MRM (Print Consultants) Ltd., Reading
Printed in England by J. W. Arrowsmith Ltd., Bristol

INTRODUCTION

Most people do not believe in ghosts. Personally I do, because I once saw one. Imagination? If so, whatever I saw was also in the imagination of my dog.

It was in the Christmas school holidays, when I was about thirteen, and we had taken our collie dog for a walk in Hyde Park. My mother was an enthusiastic collector of antiques, and she knew some of the proprietors of the London antique shops quite well.

On this occasion, she wanted to go to a shop in Wigmore Street, and I went with her, the dog on a lead. I remember that we went all over the premises, which had obviously been a private house in earlier days. On going upstairs, my mother and the owner of the shop immediately started looking at a piece of furniture, with their backs to me and to the dog.

Suddenly, I heard the dog growling, and I noticed that his hackles were rising. Looking up, I saw the figure of a woman in a grey dress, 18th century in style, glide across the floor, and disappear through a closed door. I must have said something, or else my mother heard the dog growling, as both she and the owner of the shop turned round. I explained what I had seen, and we searched the premises, but, of course, we saw nothing more. The proprietor, hearing my description of the figure, said that she had often been seen by members of his staff, although he personally had never met her.

The fact is, that for several generations, members of my family have been interested in what we now call the paranormal, and some of them have had strange experiences. I was, therefore, brought up not to scoff at the occult, but to accept that there were sometimes happenings which did occur, but which were quite inexplicable. My sighting of this ghostly figure, when I was in my 'teens, removed any remaining doubts.

Over the years, I have come across countless instances of events which seem to defy the accepted scientific laws of nature. So, if ghosts do exist, what are they? They certainly cannot be written off as figments of the imagination, which is the most popular explanation. If they were, how can one account for the many instances of total strangers experiencing the same phenomena at different times?

Ghosts, I think, must be fitted into the whole range of paranormal phenomena which still puzzle us. The word *paranormal* has only recently found its way into modern dictionaries, and its meaning is described as *not susceptible to normal explanations*. There are a great many odd happenings which fall into this category, and they are all inexplicable in our present state of knowledge. Glimpses into the future, generally quite trivial, mysterious rappings on walls and furniture, the sound of footsteps, locked doors being opened, and doors locked from inside, weird sounds, the voices of unseen people, smells both pleasant and unpleasant, sudden drops in temperature, and inexplicable feelings of unease in certain places. All of these, as well as ghosts, can be classified as paranormal.

There are, of course, a great many theories about ghosts, which it is as well to consider. I have already mentioned the idea that a heightened imagination may be the explanation. Some so-called ghostly happenings can probably be written off as due to natural causes, such as a trick of light, a factor which one must bear in mind in assessing the truth or otherwise about a ghost story. But many ghost stories cannot be simply explained away. There is probably a grain of truth in the traditional view that some ghosts are the spirits of dead people, unable for one reason or another to rest. I have come across a number of instances where hauntings have ceased after prayer or exorcism. I have also heard ghosts described as the cinema screen of time, and there does seem to be something in the idea that some people after death leave a kind of photographic negative on the atmosphere, visible as a positive print or film to certain people under certain conditions. In support of this theory it is a fact that many ghosts always keep to their appointed routes, irrespective of structural alterations to floors or walls, or even complete re-building. Then there is the suggestion that time, as we know it, is a man-made affair, of past, present and future, and that there are other dimensions in time, criss-crossing one another, which in our present state of knowledge we don't yet understand.

This latter theory would certainly account for tantalising glimpses into the future, which some people occasionally experience, usually in dreams, and also of course for ghostly sightings.

I have heard many well-authenticated stories of the vision of a person at the moment of his or her death by someone very close to the person who has died. This must, I think, be an extension of what we know as telepathy, or communication between minds. It is significant that these sightings do not recur.

I have not mentioned poltergeists or, more strictly, poltergeist phenomena, which certainly can be included under the heading of the paranormal. Today, the traditional view that such activities are the work of mischievous spirits is generally discarded in favour of the theory that some people, often young and emotionally disturbed, can quite unconsciously generate forces over which they have no control. I have no doubt at all that such phenomena do exist, having myself had objects thrown at me, when I was alone in a room. As far as I know, I was not particularly emotionally disturbed at the time, nor was this factor present in a fairly recent local case, which is described in full in the Appendix.

Finally, to conclude the list of paranormal phenomena, one must mention astral projection of a living person. In Scotland, to see the wraith of a living person is supposed to be very bad luck. Be that as it may, several members of my family once saw the ghost of a neighbouring laird, who subsequently served gallantly in World War I, and came through unscathed. My own family, however, was decimated in the war which broke out soon after the event.

Having over the years made a study of paranormal phenomena in Berkshire and elsewhere, I have come to a few tentative conclusions. First, that not all phenomena have the same cause. Secondly, that there is more than one category of what we term ghosts. By far the greatest number of sightings seem to be of imprints left on the atmosphere, always seen in the same places. But there are also what our forebears would have called earthbound spirits. There must be some surviving element, after death, of certain persons who do not seem able or wish to leave the earthly plane.

I cannot explain the seemingly pointless nature of most hauntings. There are surprisingly few echoes of crime and violence, and great historical dramas have left little imprint.

Then, it is clear that comparatively few people are susceptible to occult or paranormal phenomena. Possibly, the gift, if it may be so termed, is inherited. This certainly seems to have been the case in my own family in which I am the third generation to have had psychic experiences. Perhaps this may explain why a house, reputed to be haunted by one set of occupants, may appear to be ghost-free on changing hands.

One question which I am often asked is why do ghosts always seem to appear in drab colours, or in white? In this book, there is only one instance of a very brightly clad figure, and I have no idea of why this should be the case. I am also asked about modern ghosts. Are there any? There is not much evidence, but the reader will come across a few relatively recent incidents. On the whole, ghosts, like old soldiers, seem in time to fade away.

On one count we may be quite certain. The evidence for many hauntings is very slender, but once a story has gained credence, one can be sure that it will endure and become exaggerated over the years. Nonetheless, there is overwhelming testimony to genuine ghostly and other paranormal phenomena, however little we may be able to explain why or how they occur.

In this book I have tried to put together, alphabetically, the results of my researches into the paranormal in the county of Berkshire. Wherever possible, I have given the sources of my information, but in some cases people who have helped me have been unwilling to be named. Other people have been equally reluctant for me to dis-close the identity of houses in which they have had paranormal experiences. This is perfectly understandable, and I have tried to respect their wishes.

Angus Macnaghten
Ascot 1986

ARBORFIELD

Hall Farm stands on the site of Arborfield Hall. The ghost of a girl has been seen in the grounds. She is believed to be a girl who cut her throat under an oak tree. She had been seduced by the owner of the house, who promised to marry her but instead deserted her and married someone else.

White's Farm on the Swallowfield Road at Arborfield was at one time haunted by the ghost of the farmer's wife, reputed to be a witch, and certainly very mean. Soon after her death (this all happened in the 18th century) there were several reports of a prowling figure being seen on a lonely stretch of road on dark nights. The figure would wring its hands and groan, finally disappearing into a pond by the roadside. Seven clergymen were summoned to keep vigil, and we are told that, when the figure emerged from the pond, they chanted in unison, continuing to do so until it descended again into the depths. The villagers then lowered a huge flat stone over the spot in the pond where the figure disappeared. The hauntings then ceased.

About a hundred years later there was a tail-piece to the story, when a gang of labourers were sent to clean out the pond. At the bottom they found a flat stone, and they were about to remove it when the foreman, presumably a local man, hurriedly told them to leave it where it was. When, in the present century, the pond was finally filled in, the stone was left in place. This is typical local legend which has been handed down from generation to generation.

The reference to seven clergymen taking part in the 'laying' of the ghost is interesting. I have read elsewhere of a practice used in Berkshire to lay a ghost. A peaceful spot would be chosen, and no less than thirteen ministers of religion would stand around and read something from the Bible, six reading forwards and seven backwards, until the ghost was conquered. This practice was described by an old woman at the beginning of the present century, but she did not explain how the participants would have known when to stop, as I am sure that no self-respecting ghost would have hung about in the midst of such a gabble!

Marsh gas has often in the past given rise to stories of phantom figures, and the legend of the headless white lady, riding a white palfrey, emerging from the Rectory Marsh at another nearby village, Barkham, may well have derived from this. But what of Barkham's headless soldier who is said to have patrolled the Barkham Road? I find it odd that both of Barkham's alleged ghosts should be without their heads.

ASCOT

Children are usually very credulous, and they enjoy frightening one another with ghost stories, so it is not surprising that many schools have the reputation of being haunted. A schoolmistress called Margaret Clarke is said to have committed suicide at Heathfield School near Ascot and her ghost is supposed to haunt that part of the building, but I have no definite evidence that she has ever been seen.

There is a house called Tall Trees near the racecourse which is said to be haunted by an Admiral Sullivan who has been seen gazing out of his library window. Here, too, there is no report of a recent sighting, but the late Mrs. Dorothy Leathart, who had lived in Ascot all her life, was quite emphatic about the truth of the story.

Fernbank Road in North Ascot was the unlikely scene of poltergeist activity some ten years ago. The word is a German one, meaning 'mischievous spirit', and certainly what happens lives up to this description as the disturbances can be noisy, destructive and alarming. Usually, but not always, there are young children in the house, not necessarily at all emotionally disturbed, and there seems some unconscious connection between them and the strange forces.

In the Fernbank Road case, this family, consisting of mother, father and two small boys, had been plagued with inexplicable happenings. First, lights flashed on and off but the Electricity Board, when summoned, could find nothing wrong. Articles were thrown about the house and, most inexplicable of all, the cars, though locked, were moved during the night. One theory as to the cause of these disturbances was the presence of a wooden figure which came from Nigeria. When it was taken away for a few days over the Christmas holidays there was complete peace, but the activities started again as soon as the figure was returned to the house. The owner's wife was subsequently kind enough to send me a detailed account of these events, which covered the period Christmas 1974 until early in 1976, and this is reproduced in the Appendix.

My own view of poltergeist activity is that it is caused by some kind of human force of mind over matter, which only a very few people can control. I believe that this force is called psycho-kinesis and that it is generated quite unconsciously by certain people. On the whole, poltergeist phenomena are more alarming than destructive, though this is not always the case. I remember once in Scotland having objects thrown at me, and I was quite terrified, although no damage was done. I remember, too, that in my first Windsor home some friends and I were once persuaded to try to make a heavy table levitate itself. The table certainly did give a terrific lurch, which made us so alarmed that we stopped.

One of Ascot's most attractive 'period' houses is Old Huntsman's House, which is said to be haunted by a phantom dog. A lady told me that she once saw what she described as a 'great big woolly-looking dog' going into one of the bedrooms.

She thought that it might be a bob-tailed sheepdog belonging to one of the neighbours, but when she entered the room it was empty. Subsequently the dog was often heard at night barking in the passage. On another occasion, the young son of some former occupants came down to breakfast one day and enquired about a man in a red coat whom he had seen in his room the previous night. Presumably the ghostly figure had been wearing a (hunting) pink coat.

The wife of the present owner of a large late 19th century house in Ascot has told me that she once saw the ghost of a previous owner, who had died some years before. He was standing in the hall and just vanished in front of her eyes. Although the atmosphere has been improved by modernisation and redecoration, she feels that there is still 'something' there. A baby has been heard crying in an upstairs empty room, and once when there was no wind, all the doors suddenly slammed, much to the alarm of two ladies in the house.

A late Victorian house in Brockenhurst Road, South Ascot, has a sinister reputation and, possibly for that reason, it has often been up for sale. Although the exact details have been forgotten, there is a story of a child dying there in mysterious circumstances. One lady who went over the empty house some years ago was appalled by the atmosphere and vowed that she could never live there. Some people who did occupy the house for a number of years had a dog, which used to be terrified of something in the kitchen, the door of which could never be kept shut.

The Royal Ascot Hotel was a large Victorian building on the corner of the road from Windsor and the road to Bracknell. It was demolished towards the end of 1964 and the workmen engaged in its demolition were housed for a while in some of the rooms which were still intact. Their slumbers were disturbed by the stamping and snorting of a horse, not to mention ghostly footsteps along the corridors. On two occasions a phantom grey or white horse was seen, but the hauntings ceased once the site was cleared to make way for a large roundabout.

Several books on hauntings refer to the ghost of a policeman, with a terribly mutilated face, seen either on the A332 or the A329 road – accounts differ – but I have yet to meet anyone who can confirm the story.

On the whole, owners of properties are reluctant to admit that they may be haunted, but the brochure of the Berystede Hotel in South Ascot refers to a tragedy, when the building was still a private residence, in which a maid died in a disastrous fire when trying to save some jewellery. The maid, known as 'the lady dressed in blue', is said to haunt the hotel.

Finally, Mrs. Padwick, who lives in South Ascot, had an interesting experience when she and her daughter went for a walk with their dog behind Woodlands Ride, towards Swinley Forest. Both suddenly saw a postchaise, drawn by two white horses, travelling silently along a road which eventually peters out in the woods. Inside the carriage there was a woman, wearing a crinoline dress, while the driver had a cravat. A little white dog was running along behind the carriage. Mrs. Padwick's own dog was terrified.

She and her daughter have also seen a man standing in Woodlands Ride, who disappears as one approaches. This has occurred on several occasions.

Swinley Forest, then, does definitely appear to be haunted. Mrs. Doris Winchester, who used to live there, has told me that when walking her otherwise well-behaved dogs, the latter would always refuse to pass a certain spot in the forest.

BASILDON

Basildon has its share of ghosts. A Lady Fane, who lived in a house called The Grotto, is said to have been found drowned in a well inside the building, and her ghost is reputed to haunt the house. Two other ghosts are recorded: Nobes-on-his-white-horse, who lived at Tomb Farm, and Nan Carey, who was believed to be a witch.

The evidence for Lady Fane's ghost is somewhat slender. The Grotto – now the headquarters for the Institute of Park and Recreation Administration – was certainly owned by the Fane family in the 18th century, and the mention of her ghost is in an exercise book held by the Reading Public Reference Library. This reference book was compiled by a member of the Berkshire Archaeological Society, and it mentions a sighting of Lady Fane, standing on a rug before a fireplace, but there is no indication of which room was involved. The legend that Lady Fane was murdered by her husband is quite without foundation as she outlived him by many years.

Although more recent owners of the house have no evidence of hauntings, a ghost was certainly seen there during World War II by a lady, Miss Olive Smith of Twyford, at that time in the Women's Land Army and billeted in the house in 1943. She told me that in order to reach the so-called Blue Bathroom from her dormitory she had to go along a long corridor. On two occasions, during the three years she lived there, she saw the figure of a young woman with long copper-coloured hair, wearing a pale green filmy ragged long dress, come out of the wall of a small, unused room half-way along the corridor and glide into the Blue Bathroom. Other people must have seen the ghost as Miss Smith told me that the apparition was known to manifest itself during the period October to January, and always between 9 p.m. and 11 p.m.

I was also told by a Mrs. Wace, then living at Warfield, that she had once had ghostly experiences in Basildon Rectory. The manifestation was of a monk, in a brown cowl and habit, standing by her bedroom window. Her dog sensed or saw something too and was, according to Mrs. Wace, absolutely terrified.

BINFIELD

The now demolished Billingbear House (reputed to have had 365 windows) was alleged to be haunted, though Miss Violet Woods, who was ninety in 1976 and who used often to stay there before World War I, had never heard of there being a ghost there. She remembered a blackthorn which used to flower on Christmas morning, when many people from Binfield used to go and see it.

BISHAM

If I had to select a single place to qualify as the best known haunted house in Berkshire, I would probably choose Bisham Abbey, on the Thames, near Marlow.

It is not my intention to go into any great detail of the history of this extremely interesting house: let it suffice that a 13th century preceptory of the Knights Templar formed the nucleus of the present house. A House of Austin Canons, founded by William de Montacute, Earl of Salisbury in 1337, was entirely independent of the Templars' building. The latter became the home of the Salisburys. In 1539 Margaret Pole, Countess of Salisbury, was living there when she was attainted, tried and executed in the Tower of London, her only crime being that her Plantagenet blood gave her a possible claim to the throne.

After the secularisation of the Abbey, both buildings and the estate were in due course given to Henry VIII's ex-wife, Anne of Cleves, who exchanged it for a property in Suffolk belonging to the Hoby family.

BISHAM

The male members of the Hoby family were scholars and diplomats, much in favour with the Tudors, and Sir Thomas Hoby, who died in 1566, married a wife who was a scholar in her own right. She was also intensely proud and ambitious. We shall be returning to her.

In 1780, after the Hoby family had died out, the estate was acquired by George Vansittart, the family remaining at Bisham until recent years. World War I saw the Abbey in use as a hospital for Belgian soldiers, and in World War II evacuees, troops and Red Cross personnel were in turn accommodated there. It is now the property of the National Sports Centre but much of the original furnishings and paintings of the Hobys and Vansittarts remain there. Over the centuries the house has, of course, been much altered, though retaining its 16th century atmosphere.

Why should this house have such a reputation among ghost hunters? The answer seems to lie in the appalling behaviour of the formidable Lady Hoby, wife of Sir Thomas. The Hobys were, as I have mentioned, a very intelligent family, and none more so than Lady Hoby herself, so it must have been a bitter pill for her to swallow that one of her sons was an extremely stupid boy. This, at least, is the legend. We know of the birth of two sons, both of whom grew up, but there is no record at Bisham of the birth of a third son though, of course, he may well have been born elsewhere. Sceptics, however, are ready to disbelieve that he ever existed.

But to return to the legend: this son was accidentally killed by his mother, who was infuriated by his stupidity at his lessons. One version is that she beat him to death, and another that she locked him as a punishment in a small closet. Being summoned unexpectedly to join her friend, Queen Elizabeth, Lady Hoby forgot all about the boy so that when he was ultimately found he was dead.

In 1840, when major alterations were being made to the Abbey, some old copy books were discovered, and subsequently lost, but not before it had been established that they had apparently belonged to one of the Elizabethan Hoby children. Someone also noted that there were blots on every page, and many corrections, presumed to have been made by Lady Hoby. Everyone naturally jumped to the conclusion that the books had belonged to the unfortunate dunce of the family, but before they could be properly examined they disappeared, apparently having been taken away by one of the workmen.

So much for the history of the house. What of the different manifestations that have appeared there? So many accounts have already been published about them that I will confine myself to listing them rather briefly, but anyone who wishes to read about them in detail should consult Piers Compton's *The Story of Bisham Abbey*. Probably the most famous ghost story of all is that of the appearance of Lady Hoby to Admiral E. H. Vansittart, who one night was the last of the family to remain downstairs. Lady Hoby's portrait hung in the panelled room where the Admiral and his brother had been playing chess and where the Admiral, alone in the room, suddenly felt that someone was standing behind him. Turning round he recognised Lady Hoby and, glancing at the picture on the wall, he saw that the frame was empty. Not surprisingly, he fled from the room.

Guests at balls and dances at the Abbey seem to have had terrifying experiences. A Foreign Office clerk, invited to a ball, slept with his retriever in the only available bedroom and woke in the night to hear the sound of something dropping, nearer and nearer to his bed, 'a thick sort of sound, not like water'. The dog leapt on to the bed and the unfortunate man felt a cold mist creeping over him. Then he fainted. Another young man, competing at Henley Regatta, was allowed to sleep in the library. He had a fine head of hair so he was doubly alarmed that night when Lady Hoby's ghost approached him and said, 'Young man, if I but touch thee, thou wilt be bald'. We are told that he gave up rowing, and went into the Church.

A Miss Drysdale, attending a small dance at the Abbey during World War I, foolishly decided to go up to bed early. Cosily reading a book in her curtained fourposter bed, with her West Highland terrier beside her, Miss Drysdale soon fled downstairs, terrified. Unseen hands had torn the curtains off the bed, her diamond wrist-watch was flung into a corner of the room, and her toilet set and a pile of music were thrown on to the floor. The dog had meanwhile fled, and Miss Drysdale then saw the figure of a tall woman, wearing a white garment, standing between the bedposts. Asked to examine the family portraits, Miss Drysdale unhesitatingly pointed to that of Lady Hoby as her malevolent visitor.

Many people have reported feeling that they were being watched, and one resident wrote that 'the most awful noises' were often heard coming from behind the panelling in the hall.

Now that the ownership of Bisham Abbey has passed out of private hands, do the hauntings continue? I put this question some years ago to Mr. Brian Lee, the Director, and he replied, 'It is unknown to us that any hauntings have been apparent in recent years, but in some instances the imagination has run wild on occasions!'

BLEWBURY

According to the late Mr. F. M. Underhill, F.S.A., whose knowledge of the Old County of Berkshire was unsurpassed, Blewbury contains several haunted houses. The late Mr. Langford Jones, the artist and sculptor, told him how when he first came to live in the village he took lodgings for a time while his own house was being made ready for him. The cottage where he stayed was troubled by a poltergeist that used to move household objects and throw them about. As Mr. Jones was lying in bed one morning the wash-basin on the stand beside him suddenly flew across the room and dashed to pieces against the opposite wall. There was no-one else in the room at the time and Mr. Langford Jones was quite unable to explain how it happened.

BRACKNELL

Caesar's Camp, once an Iron Age fort, is a well-known beauty spot on a hill, surrounded by beech woods, and it was the scene of some strange experiences in a house there, now demolished. I was told by a lady how she and her sister had taken this house during World War II. It was a lonely spot but troops often used to pass along the foot of their garden, which was separated from the high road by a hedge of rhododendrons. One summer evening, when she and her sister were preparing for bed, they heard the sound of voices and marching footsteps. She looked out over the hedge to see the soldiers but there was nothing there, only the sound of voices and the crunch of boots.

One night the same lady woke up to find a man standing by her bedside. She had no impression of what he was wearing, only that his face was 'very striking' and that he had red hair. She was terrified, but managed to call out 'What do you want?'. The figure backed away, and vanished, her sister, hearing her voice, came to see what was the matter, and assured her that there was no-one in the house.

After her sister had left, this lady remained in the house with her son, whom she describes as having been a very serious-minded boy. He was then fourteen years old. One day he rushed, white-faced, into the house, telling his mother to bolt the door as there was a horrible man coming along the road, 'his face all screwed up funny'. His mother hurried to look out of an upstairs window from where there was a clear view of the road, but it was empty. To this day her son maintains the truth of what he saw.

The village of Easthampstead has now been swallowed up by the town of Bracknell but, like every village, at one time it had its own mill. A 17th century farmer, who owned the mill, was notoriously mean but very prosperous. One hard winter, when his neighbours were suffering, he ignored their appeals for charity, holding on to his flour in order to get the highest possible price. One stormy night he was roused by the barking of his dog and heard a knock on the farmhouse door. Peering out of the window he saw a man, dressed in rags, who begged him for some food. The farmer told him to be off or he would set his dog upon him, and returned to bed. Next morning he stumbled over the frozen body of the man in rags.

It is satisfying to learn that from that time on everything began to go wrong for the farmer, his crops failing, his cattle dying and his land flooding. To add to his misery the farm and mill were constantly haunted by a man in rags, and eventually the farmer and his family had to take to the road like beggars. Farm and mill lay deserted, going to ruin, as no-one would venture near, until eventually a group of villagers burnt down what remained of them and the haunting ceased.

BRIMPTON

The little hamlet of Brimpton, south-east of Thatcham, is supposed to be haunted by a ghostly carriage and pair. On a certain night in January the carriage is heard travelling down Brimpton Lane. When it reaches Abel Bridge, the horses can be heard plunging and the passengers screaming. The haunting is said to be the annual re-enactment of a tragedy, when a carriage was taking a party of young people to a Hunt Ball. The bridge was swept away in a storm and all the occupants of the carriage were drowned.

BUCKLEBURY

The village of Bucklebury is rich in hauntings: an evil spirit is said to waylay nocturnal travellers and chase them down the Devil's Steps. What is described as 'a grisly apparition' appears in broad daylight on the isolated common-land called Bushnell's Green; a lady in white flits along the Avenue at Beenham turning, and two monks have been seen near the medieval fishponds on the Common. The Manor House, formerly the home of the Winchcombe family, passed with the death of the last male heir in 1703 to Frances Winchcombe, who married Lord Bolingbroke. The marriage was an unhappy one and Lady Bolingbroke's ghost is said to drive through the village in a coach drawn by four black horses, and on one night of the year to sit in the drawing-room of the Old Vicarage.

CAVERSHAM

The following story was told to me several years ago by Mrs. M. Atkinson of Caversham.

At some period during World War II her father was night watchman at Rose Hill, Emmer Green, at that time the local headquarters of the Salvation Army. Mrs. Atkinson described the house as a 'big old rambling place', situated on the left-hand side of the road leading to Peppard.

Shortly after taking up his duties, her father was stoking the boiler when he heard the sound of footsteps and the tinkling of glasses. He came out to investigate and as the footsteps approached he switched on his torch. There was no-one there. The night watchman followed the sounds upstairs, along a passage, into a room, where the noise of footsteps and tinkling glasses ceased.

He told another night watchman of his experience and the latter said that he had often heard the same sounds. The invisible ghost, he said, was believed to be that of a butler, who had hanged himself on a tree outside the house.

Mrs. Atkinson's father heard the footsteps and tinkling glasses on numerous occasions, but he took no further notice of the sounds.

CLEWER

The Church of England's Children's Society used to run a children's home in a large house at Clewer, said to have belonged at one time to the (Anglican) Sisterhood of St. John The Baptist. One of the senior staff bedrooms became quite untenable and had to be turned into an office, which was used only in the daytime. The supposed cause of the haunting was the death of a nun, who hanged herself in the grounds: Miss Gladys Thompson, who once spent the night on duty in the room told me that, in spite of a large coal and wood fire, the room became icy cold, and a misty vapour hovered overhead. Miss Thompson was not thinking of the supernatural and she imagined that the mist was smoke coming from the fire, until she realised that the fire – though giving out no heat – was burning brightly and not smoking. The home was closed in recent years and the house has since been demolished.

A spare bedroom in one house at Clewer was only used in cases of emergency because of its unpleasant atmosphere. Although nothing was ever said, for fear of frightening the children or the daily help, Mrs. Helen Weston told me that she used to make the sign of the cross whenever she had to go into the room. Some years after the house had been sold, she spoke to her former daily help and asked whether she had ever felt anything odd in any part of the house. The latter at once mentioned the spare bedroom, saying that she hated going into it and that she always hurried through her work so as to get out of the room as quickly as possible.

There was no explanation for this feeling of unease, but at some period of its history there was probably a tragedy in the house, leaving an unpleasant imprint on the room in which it occurred.

COOKHAM

Cookham is reputed to have its ghosts, both ancient and modern, ranging from a headless lady in white to steps on the roof of a modern prefab, but I have not been able to obtain confirmation of any of these stories. Whiteladyes Lane is supposed to have been named after a ghostly nun who walks there, but the name is not an old one so the legend must be of comparatively recent date.

But the Common At Cookham Dean was the setting of an extraordinary experience one summer's evening in the 1920s, when a sensible, matter-of-fact lady crossed the common on her way to post a letter. On her return down one of the rides which then crossed the common, she noticed that her two dogs were frightened of something and that they were cowering behind her. Looking up, she saw the figure of a man, wearing antlers, coming out of the undergrowth which at that time covered the common. Not being afraid, she turned back down the track and followed the figure, to see it disappear into one of the three oak trees on the edge of the common. I heard this story from Mr. Desmond Ellis who lives at Cookham Dean, and who knew the lady in question. This sounds uncommonly like a sighting of *Herne the Hunter*, about whom I have plenty to say in my chapter on Windsor Castle. Cookham Dean lies on the edge of the vast tract of land once known as Windsor Forest.

DATCHET

The 'ghostly palm print' on a window pane in the old Royal Stag Inn is Datchet's main claim for inclusion in this book. According to local legend, a child died of cold one winter when waiting outside the inn for his father, a well-known drunkard, the idea being that the child put his (or her) hand on the window pane, leaving an indelible print. So much for the legend: some people claim to be able to see the print. Others do not. A macabre feature of the inn is that the floor was paved with old gravestones. The so-called print was photographed in 1979 by Mr. Richard Smith, a local resident, who stated to a reporter that there were several eyewitness reports referring to ghostly footsteps, noises and severe drops in temperature, when dogs behaved in a frightened manner. A whole series of licensees have confirmed these stories, and a young resident barman claimed that one night he had heard footsteps approaching his room, and that 'something' had pounced on him and had held him down on his bed.

ENGLEFIELD

Englefield House, probably dating from the 16th century, was badly damaged by fire in 1886, and largely rebuilt. This, however, does not seem to have removed the ghost of a former owner, Powlett Wright, which is reputed to haunt the house and the tunnel (now blocked up) under the back region of the buildings. According to the *Berkshire Village Book*, many bygone villagers have reputedly given evidence to this effect.

ETON

Since the redrawing of the county boundaries, Eton is now part of Berkshire. The old Cockpit Restaurant, a building dating from the 15th century, has been a rendezvous for generations of Etonians and their friends. At the side of the garden behind the building is one of the few remaining cockpits in this country. Most were demolished after the barbarious sport of cockfighting had been made illegal, but the Eton example survives, a reminder of the days when hardly any animal or bird was immune from the 'sportsman' and the gambler. But the Cockpit ghost has nothing in common with bloodshed and violence – a little grey lady who flits about the house.

Today, many old houses in the High Street have been adapted as antique shops and I once heard an interesting story concerning one of them. We are inclined to think of apparitions as being confined to persons and certain animals, but this is a case where the ghost – if it can be so termed – was a piece of furniture. Mr. and Mrs. Charles Toller were living above the shop, and on returning from boarding school for the holidays their fifteen year-old son went upstairs to fetch a book from the room which was used as a drawing-room. On coming downstairs he asked about a dough-bin or coffer which he had noticed under the window. His mother knew that there was nothing like that there – only a small tripod table – and suggested that he should have another look, which he did. On this occasion he did not see the coffer and was rather surprised, but not too much, as the family recognised that they had 'second sight'. His mother once told me that curious things did happen just about that time in the house. 'In the back room, where I used to sit at night – quite often alone', she said, 'I got quite accustomed to seeing the dog jump up to greet an unknown visitor, while the cat rubbed herself round unseen legs. I wished I could have seen who they were making such a fuss of.' Obviously a very friendly presence or the animals would have reacted quite differently!

Another friendly ghost in Eton is that of a doctor who was in practice there and who was noted for his fondness for children. Children of later tenants of the house – No. 117A High Street – have seen 'the litle old man in brown' and have not been at all frightened by him, wishing he would come more often.

Thomas's, the hairdressers in the High Street, is supposed to be haunted. Before being taken over by the late Mr. Thomas, the business, then known as Jeffries's, was run by a family called Betteridge. The owner's son committed suicide by cutting his throat with a razor and his ghost is said to haunt that part of the shop which is used for men's hairdressing.

Nearby, in another well-known business in the High Street, where the proprietor's family still lives upstairs, there is a story that one of them was scared stiff by the sight of a woman walking eighteen inches above the floor. Soon afterwards a surveyor from Eton College, which owns the building, informed them that the floor had at some time, in fact, been lowered eighteen inches.

This was the story as I first heard it but on checking directly with the family concerned I was given a rather different account.

The previous tenant of the business had been an elderly man, who had been knocked down and killed by a car outside the shop. He had bequeathed the contents of the house to his employees, who had taken what they wanted and had left quite a number of articles behind, which were still there when the new tenants moved in. The family was struck by the creepy atmosphere of the house and they were constantly disturbed at night by heavy footsteps on the stairs. The mother-in-law of the new proprietor came to stay and she at once complained of the noise. She was told the recent history of the business and she insisted that all reminders of the previous tenant should be destroyed. Furniture, clothing, prints and other household effects were all taken out and burnt, and the footsteps ceased.

But one night the family heard screams coming from the bedroom occupied by their nine year-old daughter. They rushed up to her room and saw *something* – quite impossible to describe – hurling itself about the room, so the family hastily took the child and left *it* still careering about. There has been no recurrence but the room is always left unoccupied unless there is an acute shortage of accommodation.

Eton College, too, has its ghosts. A very old house on the Slough Road is reputed to be haunted though details are lacking. So was one of the boys' Boarding Houses. There was one room at the back of the house, used as a spare room, from which on frequent occasions the sounds of somebody moving about and opening and shutting drawers were heard, but when one opened the door and went in the noises immediately stopped and there was nothing unusual to be seen. The housemaster's wife, Mrs. Hubert Hartley, used to sleep in the next room, and she was often aware of what she could only describe as a miasma coming through the wall. This house, Coleridge House, in Keate's Lane, has now been demolished and the site is occupied by an extension of another Boarding House.

According to Mrs. Hartley (who heard the story from the then Dame), a service of exorcism was once held in Coleridge House, though the details are obscure. It must have taken place in the 1920s, when Mr. Huson was Housemaster there. Tradition associates (Nancy) Lady Astor with the affair, although her family consider it most unlikely. Two of her sons were at Coleridge House and they never felt anything uncanny there. Lady Astor was a firm believer in Christian Science and her family is of the opinion that she would never have called in ministers of religion of another church. It would be interesting to know if Dr. M. R. James, who was Provost of Eton at the time, and a classic writer of ghost stories, played any part, and I should naturally be glad to hear from anyone who can throw any light on the story.

'Spirit' photographs can easily be faked, but two instances of such photographs at Eton bear recording. After the death of Mr. H. E. Luxmoore, a very famous Eton Master, in the mid-1920s, a small pavilion was put up in what is known as Luxmoore's Garden, which he had created; and the occasion was attended by twenty or thirty of his friends. A photograph was duly taken, facing the pavilion and the dais on which were dignitaries, with the backs of the assembled company in front of the camera. The photograph, when developed, showed clearly the back view of Mr. Luxmoore among the guests, an unmistakably picturesque figure even from the back, with flowing white hair, a white stock and frock coat.

Another account of the same incident was sent to me by the son of an Eton Master, Mr. Streatfield, whose wife was present on the occasion. He wrote 'My mother was present at the little ceremony. Shortly afterwards she met Mr. Mundy, the photographer from Kissack's in the High Street. In some excitement he asked my mother to go to his shop. There he showed her his recently developed photograph of the ceremony with the summer-house in the background. My mother at once recognised the very familiar figure of Mr. Luxmoore, standing a little aside from the official group – evidently quite unmistakable with his characteristically hunched shoulders and wearing a short cape, as was evidently his regular custom'.

Another photograph taken at Eton contains two shadowy figures, which may possibly be ghostly imprints. The late Mr. C. R. N. Routh was a Master at Eton from 1920 to 1958 and a keen amateur photographer. On one occasion, taking photographs for the College photograph archives, he took a picture from the organ loft of College Chapel of the altar and the old east window. When it was developed he noticed two shadowy figures in the print. They were obviously an elderly couple and they stood gazing at the altar with their backs to the camera. The old man was leaning on a gnarled stick, and his wife had a slight stoop. Mr. Routh was convinced that no-one went in or out of the Chapel during the whole time that he was there, and he was quite satisfied that it was neither a trick of lighting nor a case of double exposure, as the figures were standing so exactly in proportion to their surroundings.

Eton College's most famous ghost is that of Jane Shore, mistress of Edward IV, who dissuaded her royal lover from destroying the school founded by his Lancastrian rival, Henry VI. When she was out of favour, imprisoned and penniless, the Provost and Fellows secured her release and gave her a room in Lupton's Tower, which faces the School Yard, where she lived until her death in 1526. According to legend her ghost, commonly known as the Grey Lady, haunts the Cloisters and Lupton's Tower.

A few years ago, an assistant editor of the *Eton College Chronicle* saw a figure which may have been that of Jane Shore. One winter evening, passing the Porson Library, just underneath Lupton's Tower, he saw that a beam of light from the tower was illuminating the figure of a lady clad in a long dark medieval dress. At first he took no notice, but then he saw that 'though her legs were moving she was not going anywhere'. Let him tell the story in his own words. 'Naturally I was scared, and decided not to return to my house by my usual route which was through the graveyard. Instead, I chose to go round by the Brewhouse Gallery. There was a board lying between Brewhouse Yard and School Yard. As I walked over it, it made its usual clumping sound. I walked hastily onwards. About five seconds later I heard the same clumping sound. The woman was following me. I ran towards Baldwin's Bec, my pulse beating fast. Before entering the door I looked round. I saw a sudden white flash and whatever had been following me disappeared.'

The Vice-Provost's Lodge lies off the old Cloister of the College and may very well be haunted. Between 1956 and 1959 much of the house was used as storerooms, but a Mr. and Mrs. Marsland occupied the second floor of the building. The first signs that the house was haunted came when Mrs. Marsland heard someone coming quietly upstairs. She thought that it must be a shy boy coming to get something signed, for each time she called to the person to come on up he took fright and disappeared. Gradually Mrs. Marsland became used to hearing this visitor and did not call out. If she pretended to take no notice it would have the courage to come further and further up the stairs, until it would finally stand at the kitchen door and watch while she was preparing a meal.

Occasionally she was able to catch a glimpse of it out of the corner of her eye. It was, she says, a figure of about five feet six inches tall, dressed in a long, dark grey medieval costume of rough woollen material. She did not find it violent or even anti-social, but instead rather companionable. 'There was a very nice atmosphere when it was there', she wrote. The figure came at all times of the day, and when she did look round to see it the figure just vanished. Mrs. Marsland thinks that what she saw was the ghost of a boy who had died several centuries ago, but nothing has been seen or heard of this shy ghost since the house again became official residence of the Vice-Provost.

The ghost of a man who appears to be in fancy dress is sometimes seen in Eton, though nobody knows who he is or why he continues to haunt the place.

Some years ago, two sisters were walking one evening from Eton College towards Slough when, ahead of them, one of them saw a man walking towards them. 'He was swinging along the road', the late Mrs. B. J. Corden, of Datchet, told me, 'and seemed to be in fancy dress – like the advertisement for Sandeman's Port – with a black cloak and a broad felt hat. Suddenly he disappeared through a bricked-up doorway.' A few days later she revisited the scene, and confirmed that there was no doorway where she had seen him vanish. Many years later Mrs. Corden read an account of another sighting of this ghost, which she immediately recognised, but I have not been able to trace the book in question.

A less permanent ghost was once heard at the other end of the little town, at the Windsor and Eton Waterworks on Tangier Island. This event occurred during World War II. The Works were manned twenty-four hours a day and it was the custom of the night-shift man to make a cup of tea about midnight, a fact known to the Eton police, one of whom would make the Works a point of call at about that time. The entrance to the mess-room was protected by a blast wall but the arrival of the policeman would always be heard by reason of the ticking of the free-wheel of his bicycle.

One night, the attendant heard the free-wheel as it approached, accompanied by the measured tread of the policeman, so he put the kettle on. The noises grew louder and stopped. No-one came in so he went out, looked up and down the path leading to the mess-room, only to see no-one. The incident was repeated the next night and the attendant told his experience the following morning to the man who came to relieve him. 'Didn't you know? Old Sergeant ——— died a couple of nights ago' came the reply.

Another haunting in Eton which was very apparent in the 1940s was in a house opposite the Cockpit in the High Street. At that time the actress Barbara Cochran was living there with her late husband, Jack Minster, the well-known stage director, and they shared the house with an amiable but noisy ghost called Mrs. Hester.

The little house is tall, and dates from the reign of Queen Anne, but the ghost was that of a comparatively recent occupant. Mrs. Hester had died at a great age and the house had then belonged to a local dentist. From him it had passed to Miss Cochran and her family. Mrs. Hester's ghost was never seen but she would be heard walking about in her old bedroom – she had been a heavy woman – and the door of this bedroom could never be kept shut. She used to be heard hurrying up and downstairs and would push past people on the stairs, her skirts rustling, like the wind. The family and their daily help became quite used to this and to the banging of doors, but some people would refuse to stay in old Mrs. Hester's bedroom.

Another haunted house in the High Street is the Three Tuns

Inn. The former landlord, Vic Strangewick, and his wife both considered the house to have a ghost in it as they had felt a ghostly customer push them aside, when serving behind the bar. The next landlord, Mr. Bert Matthews, a former professional boxer, policeman and private detective, did not believe the story until his wife told him that she had seen the door handle to the empty upstairs quarters turn. Both, too, experienced the gentle push of something unseen moving along the bar.

Their cleaner, Mrs. Metcalfe, knew nothing about the haunting, until one morning when cleaning the public bar she glanced through to the little 'middle' bar a few feet away and saw a figure – in modern clothes – at the bar. This figure suddenly faded away. Three evenings earlier two customers, sitting at a table, had had an alarming experience, of which Mrs. Metcalfe knew nothing. Suddenly one of their pint pots of bitter rose vertically and tipped over one of them. It then smashed on the floor. Mr. Matthews tried unsuccessfully to see if the effect could be repeated by an accidental tipping of the table. He maintained: 'It just could not be done – and in any case it was virtually impossible for a pint pot to be smashed by merely being dropped on the floor.'

GINGE

The Manor House at Ginge, near Wantage, was in the county of Berkshire at the time when it was the country home of Rowland Prothero, first Baron Ernle, who died in 1937. When visiting the manor, Lord Ernle used to bring staff with him from London and it was always necessary to persuade them that they need not be concerned if they should see anything unusual. There was, in fact, a family joke that no-one should be afraid of the ghost, who was named Butt or Tubb.

Lord Ernle once had an extraordinarily vivid dream about two men, whom he understood to be brothers, sitting at a large oak table in the middle of an old flagged kitchen, which might very well have been the kitchen of the manor house before modernisation. One of the men was a big, burly fellow, the other thin and foxy. In his dream Lord Ernle saw them quarrelling furiously and he believed that one was about to murder the other, when he woke up, but he could not recapture the scene again after returning to sleep. As the legend attached to the ghost was that it was one of two brothers, killed in a fratricidal quarrel, Lord Ernle may possibly have caught a glimpse of the affair.

No description of Butt or Tubb appears to have been recorded, and as Lord Ernle himself never saw the ghost there is no proper evidence to link the haunting with his dream.

To-day, Ginge Manor would appear to be free of ghosts. As sometimes happens, changes of ownership, structural alterations or modernisation seem to dispel these forces of the occult, perhaps by upsetting vibrations, the nature of which we do not understand.

HARE HATCH

I was told an extremely interesting story by a lady who lived in part of a Georgian house at Hare Hatch. The house had been divided horizontally, she occupying the ground floor. One night, a visitor staying with her went to bed in the spare room and was amazed suddenly to see in front of her a dinner party in progress, the diners in Edwardian dress. She was suddenly spotted by the ghosts, who looked at her in horror, and vanished. Only on the following morning, when she told her hostess of her experience, did she learn that she had been sleeping in the original dining-room.

Another friend slept in the same room, with her dog, which suddenly dived onto the bed, terrified. There was the noise of men and horses outside, and a man, dressed in riding clothes, came into the room. He put his hand out and vanished. Other people in the house that night heard the sound of men and horses.

HOLYPORT

My cousin, Daphne Burbury, used to live in an old manor house at Holyport, Lynden Manor, which was badly haunted in one part. However firmly one bedroom door was shut, it would always open in the night, and my cousin's mother, who was definitely psychic, once saw a figure standing at the door. Unfortunately, she did not write down an account of her experiences so the details have been forgotten. The house was subsequently the home of the Marquess of Milford Haven.

HURLEY

I have always been interested in the stories of the helpful ghosts at Ladye Place, Hurley, as my family knew the owners, Lieut. Colonel and Mrs. C. N. Rivers-Moore, whose activities and excavations seem to have brought them to the surface.

In the 12th century Ladye Place was the Priory of St. Mary, a cell of the Benedictine Abbey of Westminster, but most of the Priory buildings were destroyed in the 16th and 17th centuries and the house was twice rebuilt, first in 1600 and again in 1903. Colonel Rivers-Moore bought the house and twenty acres of land in 1924. He was naturally interested in its history and particularly in the legend that Edward the Confessor's sister, Editha, was buried there.

His brother-in-law, a doctor, was once staying in the house, and he had a curious experience which started the family off on a decade of excavations. Briefly, he felt that he had spoken in the dining-room to a monk in a brown habit. The dining-room was a fine one, marred by an inferior fireplace, and in his 'vision' the doctor believed that the monk had spoken to him, advising that the fireplace should be taken out. As there were already builders working in another part of the house, the removal of the fireplace was quite a simple undertaking, and this revealed another which presumably dated from the 1600 rebuilding.

Many visitors to the house and grounds saw ghostly monks at one time or another, and the family engaged in a series of table rapping sessions, after a friend who had practised automatic writing advised the emptying of a lost well. Table rappings, after a false start, indicated the site of the ancient well, which was partially cleared but owing to the water level it was never possible to complete this.

And so the excavations continued, directed by the advice received through table rappings. Old fireplaces, hidden foundations and a host of objects were found, but never the tomb of Editha. When the excavations finally ceased in 1944 and the house and estate were sold, the ghosts appear to have decided that their work, too, was finished, and to have departed.

This account is taken from Colonel Rivers-Moore's own writings and what he told my family, but I was not aware until recently that he was an expert conjuror, being a first cousin of Noel Maskelyn, of the famous 'Maskelyn and Devant' partnership.

He made no secret of his ability and gave local conjuring shows, when he performed many of the Maskelyn and Devant stunts with ease. Mr. F. M. Underhill, who knew him well, told me that he attended at least one of the séances at Ladye Place, when there were knocks on the walls and ceiling and table-turning. The room was in semi-darkness but Mr. Underhill, who had seen Colonel Rivers-Moore perform baffling magical stunts, was not convinced that the show was not another of his conjuring tricks. Certainly his skill as a conjuror must make one suspicious of his claims to 'spirit guidance'. Possibly the long-term efforts at Ladye Place to 'pierce the veil' – whether aided by trickery or not – can very well have stirred up psychic phenomena, which would explain the phantom monks. But the site was so full of medieval remains, above and below ground, that any form of excavations would have yielded results, whether with guidance from 'the beyond' or not.

To-day, the house is at peace, and the events during Colonel Rivers-Moore's exciting tenure must remain a mystery.

LANGLEY

Now that Slough and much of its surroundings have been transferred from Buckinghamshire to Berkshire, it is possible to include an interesting story which I heard some years ago about Ditton Park, now the Admiralty Compass Observatory.

Ditton Park falls into the Stately Home class, and was one of the country seats of the Dukes of Buccleuch. We used to know an old lady, living in Datchet, with the very grand name of Lady Mabel Cholmondeleley, though she herself was living in what might be called reduced circumstances. The story about Ditton Park which she told us was that, when major rebuilding was being undertaken, some church plate was found, concealed in a wall. This implied the existence of a chapel in the house, although there was no trace of one to be found. Some little time later one of the gardeners raking up leaves in the park was astounded to see a funeral procession crossing the grounds. The impression of the figures which he saw was quite distinct and he subsequently described their clothing as 'medieval', implying at least that they were unlike anything with which he was familiar.

The gardener watched the procession as it moved slowly forward to the place where the coffin had rested. He had the good sense to mark the spot, and subsequent excavations revealed it to be the site of a chapel. I have tried without success to obtain confirmation of this story from other sources and can only repeat that old Lady Mabel was emphatic that it had occurred. Lady Mabel died in 1944.

A much more recent and much publicised case of haunting happened at the Almshouses near Langley Church. During World War II some of them were used to house young families evacuated from London, something which was much resented by one of the old inhabitants, a Mrs. Briggs. The houses, she said, were for the benefit of the old people of the parish and she vowed that, if she were to die, she would haunt them until they were restored to their proper use.

Mrs Briggs died, and the hauntings began. Let me quote the story in the words of my informant who personally knew Mrs. Briggs. 'She (Mrs Briggs) did exactly this, scaring the wits out of the young couple installed in one of the houses. There was also evidence of poltergeist activities, such as the bedclothes being pulled off during the night, with an old lady, fully described as to her dress, standing at the foot of the bed: also a heavy bookcase being moved about. These happenings got so bad that a book and bell service was held, and after that it all stopped.'

What does one make of such stories? I wrote to the Vicar of Langley for his comments but he stated that he knew nothing about the event.

MAIDENHEAD

Maidenhead seems to have three reputed ghosts which haunt Littlewick, though I have no evidence of recent sightings. They are 'Dorcas Noble', 'The White Lady' and 'The White Dog of Feens'.

More recently, a Victorian house was bought and swiftly vacated by a Chinese family, who claimed that dead people returned in the night. Rather understandably, Hangman's Corner, the site of an old gibbet, near Maidenhead Thicket, has a sinister reputation, and some horses refuse to pass it.

Burchetts Green, too, has its ghosts. The notorious highwayman, Claude Duval, is said to haunt the area, and two houses, Woodlands and Burchetts Green House, are said to be haunted, though in neither instance are the present owners aware of anything unusual in their homes.

There are rumours of a house at Littlewick Green which was supposed to have been haunted by the ghost of a little girl, known as Nellie. However, she was never seen again after a religious service had been held in the house, so one hopes that her spirit is at rest.

The recent acquisition by the late Mrs. Laura Ashley of Braywick House for the headquarters of her flourishing company has drawn attention to the history of this stately home. Built in 1675, and later enlarged by the Adam brothers, the house has had a long history of hauntings. Footsteps are often heard in the empty attic rooms and there is a legend of a lady, dressed in white, who walks through the front door and up the stairs, leaving the house by the east window. According to a recent report in *The Daily Telegraph*, a man 'in strange costume' appears on the stairs.

NEWBURY

Many of the hauntings associated with Newbury and the surrounding villages are linked by tradition to the two great battles in the Civil War which were fought there. I am most grateful to

Miss Helen M. Purvis of Newbury and to Mr. Ray Bryant of the (*Reading*) *Evening Post* for drawing my attention to these stories.

Some twenty years ago, two sisters living at Biggs Cottage, Enborne were convinced that the Earl of Essex who lodged in the cottage overnight before the First Battle of Newbury in the Civil War, had appeared in a bedroom, but the ladies were not alarmed. This seems to have been one of those rare appearances of a ghost of a notable person. At various times the apparition was seen by both sisters, who described the man as wearing a flat cap.

There is a local tradition that a sentry appears at the corner of the road by this cottage on the anniversary of the eve of the battle. A lady who used to exercise her daughter's horse around the Enborne lanes had the utmost difficulty in persuading the animal to pass the cottage. It behaved as if there was something in the ditch, though the lady herself could see nothing.

The recently demolished Cope Hall at Enborne also had a reputation for hauntings, both in the house and grounds. The lane, with its dark high banks, featured in some of the worst fighting of the battle in 1643 and is said to have been heaped with bodies of the slain. No wonder that the atmosphere is considered 'spooky'. Cope Hall itself was reputedly the scene of a murder, a clergyman having killed his wife, leaving behind a strange atmosphere. People passing the spot would suddenly feel very cold. At one time a service of exorcism was held in the house.

Enborne House itself appears to be haunted, as many residents have reported strange noises such as clankings and rattling chains.

Falkland Garth at Wash Common is, according to tradition, the house to which Lord Falkland was brought after he had been struck down during the first Battle of Newbury. A pet dog of the Henstock family, who lived in the house, used to refuse to sleep in the kitchen, and the family cook, described as a cheerful extrovert, not given to imagining things, once saw Lord Falkland's ghost. Apart from herself the house was empty, and she had locked up after finishing her work when she felt that someone was standing behind her. Turning round she saw 'a short man, dressed in black', who quickly vanished. Later, on being shown a portrait of Lord Falkland, she recognised it as of the man she had seen.

A lady once told me that she had often visited this house and that there was a corner of the hall which was shunned by the family dogs. Could this have been where Lord Falkland's body had lain?

I have kept a letter from an old friend, Lieut. Colonel John Ramsay-Fairfax, who has since died and who knew of my interest in the paranormal. In it he wrote: 'A school-friend of mine told me that he had had an aunt living near Newbury. She was stone deaf but one Sunday, when the family had been having lunch with her, she went upstairs to rest. At about three o'clock she suddenly came rushing downstairs, calling out that there must be an accident or something dreadful happening outside. Couldn't they hear the shouting, horses neighing, even what sounded like cannon fire? They had quite a job calming her down, and had heard nothing, but later on they discovered that the date was the anniversary of the Battle of Newbury in the Civil War. And the aunt otherwise remained stone deaf!'

Bussock House (now demolished) at Winterbourne was the scene of a Civil War tragedy. The daughter of Philip Weston, a Cavalier, was in love with a Roundhead officer. During the second battle her father arranged a signal, to let the girl know how they fared. If he was killed, she would hear one trumpet blast; if her lover was killed, two trumpet blasts. If both were killed, the trumpet would sound three times. The girl waited in the garden and when she heard three trumpet blasts she fell, or threw herself, down the well. Her ghost is supposed to haunt the neighbourhood.

Another ghost in the same area is said to be that of a Mr. Philip Henshaw, who was killed in 1760 when his horse ran away with him down Bussock Hill.

Newbury itself also has its hauntings. A cafe in Northbrook Street is haunted by a Doctor Watson who lived there and died about a hundred years ago. His ghost has often been seen passing up and down the staircase; an old gentleman, dressed in black and carrying a little black bag. A piano can also sometimes be heard playing at the top of the building, the sound coming from a room which was sealed up many years ago.

There have been reports of a man walking late at night in Newbury Broadway, who suddenly disappears, and a Quaker Lady is said to have been seen in Cheap Street late in the evening. Significantly, the Quaker burial ground was on the spot now occupied by a multi-storey car park in Market Street.

Two hauntings seem to be associated with children. A furniture and upholstery business occupied the site of what is now the S.E.B. showroom, and the family who owned it reported unaccountable happenings, such as finding doors and windows open when it was known that they had been shut and fastened. They also heard the crying of a child in a back room, possibly the unhappy echo of a pupil attending a school which used to be there. The Watermill Theatre is reputed to be haunted by a child. First a fulling mill and later a corn mill, children may very well have been employed there, and there is one theory that a child may have been injured or killed by being caught in the machinery. Whatever the explanation, the ghost of a little girl appears in the upper rooms and theatre staff will not go there alone.

OAKLEY GREEN

The late Dr. Esther Rickards, O.B.E., was one of the most down-to-earth people I have ever met, so I was particularly interested to hear of a haunting in an old 16th century farmhouse, Tarbay Farm, which had been the home for two generations of her family. The ghost was apparently that of an Elizabethan nurse, who was devoted to children, as her presence was only felt when there were young people living in the house. She must have been brought up to consider draughts very dangerous as in cold weather she would always close the windows. Sometimes a member of the family might say: 'It is so cold, I am going upstairs to close the windows', only to find that they had already been shut. Today, there are no children in the house so the haunting has ceased, temporarily at least.

On hearing this story, I immediately thought of the case of Mrs. Sibell Penn at Hampton. Mrs. Penn was the devoted foster mother to the sickly King Edward VI and she is still supposed to haunt her old house at Hampton, but only when there are children there. The cottage which she was given on her retirement is either part of the present house or stood on the site, more likely the former, and the present owners have lived there for many years. Their daughter was just two and a half years old when they moved into the house, and on two separate occasions during the night she woke up, calling out that a 'little old lady in grey' was standing by her bedside. More recently, a friend, knowing nothing of the history of the house, was very definitely conscious of a 'presence'.

OLD WINDSOR

A number of people living at Old Windsor have had curious experiences. A lodge on an estate on Priest Hill was the home of a young couple, Mr. and Mrs. Allen, and their two babies for over two years and during this time there were frequent paranormal happenings. 'We would be in bed', wrote Mrs. Allen, 'when the downstairs door would open and someone would walk up the stairs, making a lot of noise, open the bedroom door, and where he went from there I don't know, but this happened every night'. They believed the ghost to be that of a former occupant who had committed suicide some forty years earlier by tying a lawnmower round his neck and jumping into the Thames at the foot of the hill. They never saw him, nor did they see the ghost of a girl who made her presence known by a very sweet scent and by sitting on the bed. 'The first time it happened', Mrs. Allen wrote, 'I was asleep, but my husband was awake and he was so terrified that he couldn't even move or call out to wake me up'. By using an ouija board they came to the conclusion that this girl was called Sally.

There were also poltergeist manifestations. Let Mrs. Allen continue. 'When my mother and father came to stay for weekends the bedclothes would be pulled off again and again. There were also lights all over the wall and ceiling and a carved wooden ornament was thrown across the room against a wall. In the end my father wouldn't sleep in the house. Our daughter would also tell us about the pretty lights, which we couldn't see, and as the house was set back off the road, once the bedroom lights were off it was pitch dark.

'Another incident: we had new lino in the bedroom and one night we smelt burning but could trace nothing. When we got up in the morning, from my husband's side of the bed, right across the bedroom to the door, footprints were burnt into the lino, and try as I might I could never remove them.'

Another first-hand account of a haunting at Old Windsor was sent to me by someone who had lived there thirty years ago. The haunting must have been caused by something very sad, and no explanation was ever forthcoming. This is what the former owner, Mr. Hugh Dinwiddie wrote:

'My wife and I and my wife's mother lived in Benet House at Old Windsor from August 1953 to September 1956. It was not long after we had moved into the house, which was built in about 1930, that we were aware of plaintive sounds that seemed to come from the chimney leading from the room (formerly the dining-room) which I used as my study. Thinking, perhaps, that there was a bird's nest in the chimney, we had the chimney swept but no nest was found.

'Soon afterwards while reading in my study, which had windows opening out into the garden, beyond which was a two-acre field, I heard the slightly sad bird-like sound coming, this time, from the garden. It was about four o'clock on a September afternoon and there were no doves or pigeons or people in the garden that could have made such sounds, which came momentarily and then faded.

'We then began to hear the sounds in different parts of the house, but mainly in the eastern end, in the kitchen, the pantry and in the small sitting-room next to the pantry which my wife, who is a pianist, used as a practice-room. One night in August 1954 my wife's sister, who had a spaniel dog, was staying with us, and the dog had his basket put in the pantry for the night. In the small hours of the morning we heard howling and it was found that this normally passive dog had completely chewed up a large sheep's wool slipper of mine that was kept in the pantry. It seemed that the 'sounds' were more frequently heard when visitors came to the house or when movements were taking place. On the night when, in September 1954, my wife's mother returned from a holiday in France, there were 'sounds' in the kitchen that made both my wife and myself independently call out and ask if she was all right. On going to the kitchen to turn off a tap that had started to give forth a jet of water I found there was no-one there, and the sounds ceased.

'Along the first floor of the house, and leading off a single passage, were the five bedrooms, the bathroom, linen cupboard and two lavatories. We usually used the third bedroom for visitors, which was the room above my study, and several friends complained of being disturbed in the night by 'sounds', by having the window opened, the tap in the wash-basin turned on, and by having the pillow and sheets twitched and pulled. Two such persons were visitors from Holland, and they did not have any knowledge that there might be some strange phenomena connected with the room.

'My wife and I slept in the second bedroom and at about two o'clock on All Souls Night, 2nd November 1954, we were both woken up by quite loud cooing cries from the direction of the linen cupboard at the bathroom end of the passage. I walked to the end of the passage but there was no sight or sign of substance that could explain the saddest and loudest of the sounds we had heard. These, as before, faded as I approached.

'From time to time non-traceable footsteps were heard on the uncarpeted ground floor passages of the house, and when next a clergyman friend (now a Bishop in America) was staying with us we asked him to perform an exorcism on the house. He had been one of our friends to be disturbed in the night on a previous visit and he performed a minor exorcism throughout the house and part of the garden, in which my wife and her mother and I participated. After this small ceremony no-one in the remaining one year of our residence in the house heard the plaintive sounds, nor were any of our friends who stayed in the house disturbed. At no time had the sounds been anything but sad.'

In a covering letter, Mr. Dinwiddie wrote: 'On looking back it seems we were inconsiderate to our guests, most of whose information was given to us only after the events recorded here, on the grounds that we must not be alarmed: Mrs. Joan Hewitt was such a one, and on stepping across the threshold with her mother told us afterwards of her immediate feelings that the house was in some way haunted'.

George IV's mistress, 'Perdita' Robinson, died, crippled and impoverished, in Englefield Cottage at Old Windsor, her daughter Maria Elizabeth dying aged eighteen in 1818. Both are buried in Old Windsor Church. According to local legend the daughter walks the graveyard in the early morning and at twilight, expressing her unhappiness. Whatever the truth of this story, one 'down-to-earth Yorkshireman type' of man had an uncanny experience when taking his dog for an evening walk. As he approached the wall of the churchyard, he saw a figure leaning against a wall. It seemed to be wearing a large hat but he could not tell whether it was male or female. As he got nearer he began to feel scared, but at two yards from the wall the figure vanished. He never came across anything like that again, but a former vicar told him that the area was haunted and that he could never persuade his dog to walk past a nearby house, The White Hermitage.

PADWORTH

The little road from Padworth to Reading used to be much used by local farmers on their way to market and the peaceful lane was also the scene of ghostly lights. The authority for this claim was Edward Hobbs, Parish Clerk from 1871 to 1911. The lights were visible at certain times of night along the road, resembling two yellowish carriage lamps, and they appeared to travel quickly. When almost near they just disappeared, and a strange, uncanny silence enveloped the watcher.

PURLEY

Purley Hall near Pangbourne was at one time the home of Warren Hastings, who lived there during part of the time that his long trial for alleged corruption was in progress. There he prepared his defence which finally led to his acquittal on all charges. Both his ghost and that of a grey lady or nun were said to haunt the house. Major and Mrs. Bradley, who moved there in 1961, found the atmosphere so oppressive that they arranged for a service of exorcism.

In answer to my enquiries Mrs. Bradley very kindly wrote to tell me of her experiences, and I cannot do better than to quote her letter. 'It is quite true', she wrote, 'that we did have a service of exorcism done here to rid the house of a very quarrelsome spirit, which I felt was of recent origin.

'Since when I have seen two charming ghosts, one presumably Mr. Hastings and the other a particularly charming old lady dressed in black panniered silk and wearing a white mob cap. Mr. Hastings was trotting briskly downstairs, pulling on a pair of gauntlet gloves. In both cases the ghosts, if they can be called that, gave a very friendly and happy impression, so the exorcism only removed the quarrelsome spirit and obviously left that which was friendly and good.

'I have never seen the "grey lady", although I was told by a previous tenant, who was born here about seventy-five years ago, before we bought the house, that she was said to exist in his boyhood. A famous psychometrist who visited us said that the house had a feel of great protection and a wonderful atmosphere, which indeed we have found to be the case.'

How very refreshing to read an account of ghosts who obviously like to remain in a house where they were so happy in their flesh-and-blood existence, extending their benevolence to its present-day occupants.

I remember telling this story to a group of ladies, one of whom afterwards told me that her brother had once been helping at a fête which was being held in the grounds. For some reason or other he had to go into the house, where he saw the ghost of a woman with a dark complexion, as if she had spent a long time in a hot climate. He wondered if this was the ghost of Mrs. Hastings. Later, he went back into the same room, to find that the furnishings were quite different from those which he had seen on the first occasion. He must, I suppose, have gone back in time when he saw the ghost.

READING

The Roebuck Hotel near the Thames at Reading is supposed to be haunted by the ghost of an Admiral, who died there some two hundred years ago in mysterious circumstances. The story is widely known in the neighbourhood but precise details are lacking, as, for instance, who the Admiral was. A former landlord claimed that furniture was moved about at night, that locked doors and windows were opened, and that mysterious footsteps were heard late at night. Dogs, too, were said to be unwilling to go into certain rooms, but more recently the landlord's dog has been happy to go anywhere in the hotel and there have been no unusual happenings during recent years.

A correspondent in Reading has told me of two interesting psychic experiences which she has had in the town. The first one related to a house in the Bath Road, which had been empty for fifteen years and was awaiting demolition. The lady was in a house, the side windows of which overlooked the garden of the empty house. One day, when she was cleaning the wash-basin in the upstairs bathroom, a movement in the garden suddenly caught her eye, there being a window immediately above the basin.

What she saw was the figure of a woman, very tall, dressed in a black dress which just allowed the tips of her shoes to be seen. She wore a huge white apron with a large bow at the back, and a white cap. In her hand she carried a white swan-necked jug, typically Victorian in character, and walked to the end of the garden where she held up the jug and turned on an invisible tap. Then she slowly turned and walked back to the house, up the steps, and was gone. When my informant passed the house later that day she noticed a bright blue haze of light at the back of the hall, a sign, she was sure, of a ghostly presence. The house has now been pulled down and new houses built on the site.

Her other experience was of a more contemporary nature. One night some friends had brought her by car to a spot near her flat, and she started to walk home across Berkeley Avenue, a fairly wide road. Two men were crossing at the same time. All three looked to right and left to see that no traffic was coming, and walked to the centre of the road. Suddenly a car came towards them with no lights. But before the car came closer she began to realise that it was something out of the ordinary as there was no sound of the engine. As the car came abreast of her she looked straight at the driver, a woman. Suddenly she saw her face and the colour of her hair – a beautiful red, piled up on her head like a coronet. The car itself was just a misty blue. Then it vanished. The two men apparently saw nothing.

Little has been written about the part played by Reading in the Civil War, when the town was besieged by the Roundheads and unsuccessful efforts were made by Prince Rupert and his cavalry to relieve it. But there are still ghostly echoes of the period. Mr. Jim Pettengell, late Editor of the *Reading Standard*, was one of a number of people to encounter the ghost of a Royalist courier in the leafy Warren, between Caversham and Mapledurham. It happened on a Christmas Day between the wars. Mr. Pettengell moved aside for a rider whom he could hear galloping up behind him. But as the sound of hooves pounded past he saw nothing, not even a disturbance in the puddles on the lane. How this ghostly horseman came to be identified with a Royalist courier one does not know, but another haunting – visible this time – is associated with the same period on the Caversham–Woodcote road. This is the spectre of a riderless white horse, galloping on, after its Royalist rider was shot by Roundheads.

The premises of William Smith Limited, the booksellers in London Street, Reading, are partly built on the site of a Quaker Meeting House, which William Penn, the founder of Pennsylvania, used to attend. There are well-attested accounts of sightings of the ghost of a man in Quaker dress who may or may not be William Penn, though the locals like to think so. The premises were badly damaged by fire in 1973–4. since when the ghost has apparently not been seen.

SLOUGH

Upton Court, a very old house near Slough, is supposed to have a ghost. On Friday nights, according to tradition, the ghost of a woman wearing a bloodstained nightdress appears in the grounds. For many years one of the homes of the Harewood family, Upton Court was often let, one of the tenants being the Victorian journalist, George Augustus Sala, and it was he who first recorded the story in a heavy, jocular manner. 'The servants', he wrote, 'were very particular in declaring that she wore a white nightgown richly frilled, with a large stain of blood on the left breast, and that she always walked on Friday night'. For 'upward of three hundred years' she had been 'frightening servant-maids out of their wits' and the domestics assured their master that they 'heard her crunch on the gravel of the carriage drive as she paced round the premises'. Sala was sceptical, and asked, 'Do such impalpable entities as ghosts wear boots?'

Cippenham, another hamlet engulfed by Slough, also claims a traditional type of ghost at an old house, Cippenham Place. A procession of cowled monks, carrying an empty coffin, circles the house three times on the anniversary in May of the death by drowning of an early owner. So far I have had no success in my enquiries as to whether anyone has seen the procession in recent years.

On the whole, Slough seems to be relatively ghost-free, but I have heard a strange story from a young man who shared a flat with two others in a house above a former chemist's shop. The form of haunting was footsteps on the stairs, followed by the slamming of a door. There were several cats which became very agitated when this happened, and my informant told me that the sounds seemed to occur only when one of the three occupants of the flat had some worrying personal problem.

From an entirely different source I heard that a nurse, who worked daily at a nursing home at Fulmer, had rooms above a chemist's shop in Slough, and that she often used to complain of being kept awake at night by the ghost, which walked across her room. I have no means of establishing whether or not these two accounts refer to the same house.

STANDEN

This hamlet lies just inside the Berkshire boundary, on the Hungerford to Salisbury road. I am indebted to Kathleen Wiltshire's *Ghosts and Legends of the Wiltshire Countryside* for an interesting story about a phantom lady on a phantom horse. Some thirty years ago, a Mr. Martin was giving his wife a driving lesson on this road, and at Standen they both saw a lady in white, riding a white horse, cross the road at right angles in front of them. She then appeared to be following a lane which might have been an old right-of-way, and they watched her until a curve in the lane hid her. Although none of the local inhabitants knew her identity she was well-known as 'the lovely lady on horseback'. Among those who had often seen her was the postman on his rounds, at the same spot, crossing the road to continue along the lane.

STANFORD DINGLEY

The Boot Inn, though not the oldest in the village, is reputedly haunted by a man who hanged himself in its orchard, and doors are said to close without human agency. The Old Rectory is also said to be haunted and a shrouded woman is supposed to walk in Jennets Wood at midnight.

SUNNINGDALE

People are inclined to write off Sunningdale as a place where many rich people live, and having an excellent golf course. Certainly, much of the little town is modern, and still expanding, but there are some Georgian and Regency houses in the village of Old Sunningdale. One of these in Whitmore Lane is reputed to be haunted. I have heard that when the children of the family were quite young, their clothes, piled tidily on chairs when they went to bed, would be found next morning in another room.

Another house in Sunningdale, typical of the large Victorian family houses in the area, claims a ghost dog in the garden. No-one appears to have written a description of the dog and I have not found anyone who has seen it. The house, incidentally, was at one time the home of Florence Nightingale's sister, Lady Verney. There are many recorded instances of people having psychic experiences during or after a severe illness, when one's occult faculties are perhaps more alert. I was told of a case of this kind by a lady living in a ground-floor flat in this house. She had been involved in a motor accident, and shortly after she had moved into her flat she became seriously ill, so she was certainly in a debilitated state at the time.

Whatever it was that she saw was not a proper human figure. She was in bed at the time, with her door open, leading into a passage and hall where her Cavalier King Charles spaniel was asleep in its basket, and the flat was in darkness. Something mauvy and phosphorescent glided across the floor and my friend described it as 'flowing and drifting, like a nun'. The shape – one can hardly call it a person – seemed to come out of the ground near an old back staircase which had been blocked up when the house was converted into flats. The dog must have sensed something as it whimpered in its basket. Like so many paranormal experiences, this one has not been repeated.

Doris Stainer was a well-known local figure in her own right, apart from being a sister of the film star, Leslie Howard. Her girls school, Hurst Lodge, had a very good reputation, especially on the arts side. Miss Stainer did not live in the school but had a house outside the grounds. After her death this was sold, and the new owner's wife was surprised one day to see the figure of an elderly woman sitting on her bed. The woman was wearing a blue cardigan. She then vanished. Miss Stainer's former housekeeper, who lived in a nearby cottage, confirmed that Miss Stainer was wearing a blue cardigan at the time of her death.

At one time the actress, Diana Dors, lived in a rented house, called The Pavilion, on the edge of Sunningdale. In her book, *Behind Closed Doors*, she wrote of her experiences there. She had known the previous owners, one of whom, a young pianist, had committed suicide, although he had been very happy in the house. Andrew Ray, the actor, spending Christmas in the house, saw a man, dressed in grey, enter his room and step behind the door, as if hiding. Ray thought that it was someone playing tricks and called out to him. The figure then stepped forward and brushed something which felt like a balloon on his face. Ray sat up in bed, turned on the light, but the room was empty.

Everyone in the house became aware of strange happenings. The room in which Andrew Ray had slept was usually kept empty but every morning the bedcover would be found wrinkled and crumpled.

The actress, Sandra Dorne, using another bedroom, heard knocking on her door but there was no-one there. On another occasion, a pet poodle scratched at the door of the room until its paws bled, trying to get at something which no-one could see.

Andrew Ray's daughter, then two or three years old, spoke of the nice man in grey whom she had seen several times in her bedroom, and one morning Diana Dors' two dogs, who had as usual been locked in the kitchen for the night, were found in the drawing-room, although they had no means of gaining access to it.

Great inconvenience was caused one day when the only bread knife in the house was found to be missing. It was discovered on the following day, sticking straight up out of a flower pot at the end of the garden.

According to Diana Dors, the present house was built on the site of part of a monastery, and she recalled strange sounds, like the trudge of sandalled feet going upstairs, celestial singing late at night, and many other curious incidents, all of which add up to the site being haunted. One of her friends, who did not believe in ghosts, saw the long robes and sandals of a man disappearing one night around the corner of his room.

Diana Dors and her husband, Alan Lake, later bought a modern house in Sunningdale called Orchard Manor. Five months after the actress had died of cancer her husband committed suicide, but before this second tragedy in the family their housekeeper, Mrs. Honor Webb, has stated that she frequently saw Diana Dors' ghost. After his death, Alan Lake also appeared to her on several occasions, but when she asked him what he wanted he would just disappear. Finally, Mrs. Webb consulted a clairvoyant, and the haunting stopped soon after.

SUNNINGHILL

Although much enlarged and still spreading, the village of Sunninghill is an old one and there are still some 17th and 18th century houses in the area. One early 18th century cottage, which has over the years been the subject of various alterations, is supposed to be haunted by a woman. This particular haunting bears out the theory that some ghosts are photographed on the atmosphere, as the figure has been seen crossing the drawing-room and passing through a wall where there was once a door.

Miss Jameson, a well-known local resident, who lived in the house for many years, once had a curious experience there. Having gone up to bed, she decided to come downstairs again to fetch something out of the drawing-room, and she was very surprised to see a woman sitting at a table, her hands cupped together as if she were reading a book. The figure, in modern clothes, appeared to be perfectly solid, but suddenly vanished. Three years later, at Malvern, Miss Jameson, who was staying with friends, instantly recognised another of their guests as the woman she had seen in her house, but the latter disclaimed any knowledge of ever having been there.

Sunninghill Park was, of course, once part of Windsor Forest, and any mention of a phantom horse always conjures up the story of Herne the Hunter, of whom more later.

A Mr. R. H. Kent had a very curious experience in Sunninghill Park in 1941, one night when he was on guard duty, being part of a searchlight unit based in a field. Mr. Kent was on duty on the far side of a bridlepath, separated from the Windsor to Ascot A332 road by a five-barred gate. He was on the midnight to 2 a.m. guard duty and about three quarters of an hour after beginning his duty he was amazed to hear a horse's hoofbeats in the distance, coming from the direction of Ascot. 'I was really flabbergasted', he wrote to me, 'and the noise of the pounding of hooves was terrific, as they were immediately in front of me, then they receded'. He was prepared to swear that he saw neither horse nor rider but he was ridiculed by his mates when he told them of the incident.

Mr. Kent did, however, get some comfort from the landlord of the Duke of Edinburgh public house, which is up a road immediately opposite the ride where he was on duty. After he had told his story to the landlord, the latter informed him that he had in the past heard the same account from no less than three other people.

SWALLOWFIELD

A 15th century house in this village is reputed to be haunted by an invisible presence, which is heard coming out of an upstairs room. Steps are heard coming down the stairs to the hall and crossing another room to a cupboard, where 'a sort of scuffling noise' is heard: that is how it was described to me by someone who had lived there. Not everyone, of course, heard the phantom footsteps, but the son of the house claimed once to have seen the handle turn on the door leading into the empty room at the top of the stairs.

I was told an interesting story about a haunting in the grounds of Swallowfield Park. A lady wrote to me as follows: 'One day as I was walking back from the house through the fields to catch a bus, my little dog running ahead as she always does and looking for a rabbit or squirrel, we were nearing the bridge over the river that runs through the grounds, when Peggy stopped and refused to go on. There was little time to waste so I picked her up. She was shivering and seemed reluctant to cross the bridge. By now I was on the curve of the bridge, and sitting on the wall was a man dressed in the clothes of long ago. It was twilight, and he was very clear, wearing high boots, a cloak and ruffles, and a large Cavalier type of hat with a feather plume. I felt a strange, eerie feeling, yet not of fear; or at least not as if there was evil around. We passed very close. The figure did not move and I looked straight at it. It was still there when I looked back further along the bridge. Then it moved. Waiting for no more, I hurried on into the village. A few weeks later, on meeting my friend who lives at Swallowfield Park, I asked her if the park had any history of a ghost. Her reply was that an apparition had been reported to have been seen, one by a labourer returning from work years before, and another villager had also seen one. The description was about the same as mine.'

THATCHAM

Mr. and Mrs. Patrick Ramsay, who now live at Englefield Green, used to live on a farm at Thatcham, built on the site of a moated Manor House. The first-hand account of strange happenings there is as inexplicable and pointless as any of the stories that have come my way. 'I was in the larder one day,' Mrs. Ramsay told me, 'when a woman's voice said very loudly in my ear, "Moind moy poy!" (broad Berkshire for "Mind my pie!"). There was no-one in the house except for myself. My husband was digging in the orchard.

'The corollary – although there may have been no connection –was some months later, when my mother came to stay with us. We were watching from a first-floor window the farm manager's wife pushing a pram across the farmyard and leading two small children. My mother asked "Who is the little old woman with them?" I said there was no one there, but she insisted that there was an old woman dressed in brown. I ran down to meet the group, but apparently, as I approached she vanished. This was at four o'clock on a summer afternoon. I had not told my mother of the previous incident, indeed, I had almost forgotten it, but the voice and the person were so homely that I like to think they must have belonged together.'

There are several interesting points about this story. First, that Mrs. Ramsay's mother saw the ghost of an old woman, while Mrs. Ramsay, looking at the same scene, did not. Secondly, Mrs. Ramsay's experience of hearing someone speaking to her is unusual in paranormal happenings.

The story also illustrates how ghostly tales can become distorted. The version, as I first heard it, was that Mrs. Ramsay, alone in the kitchen, turned round, to see an old woman looking at her. The figure asked, in broad Berkshire, 'Where's my rabbits?' and vanished. Fortunately, I was able to check the story with Mrs. Ramsay, and I have been able to record it exactly as it happened.

WARFIELD

This ancient parish must certainly have its ghosts but I have been unlucky in tracking them down. One house is certainly haunted. 'There is something in a room at the top of the stairs', I have been told by an estate agent who knows the house well. But the present occupant was unaware of the ghostly presence, and I was urged not to make enquiries for fear of causing alarm.

The neighbourhood of the village is said to be the scene of a curious form of haunting which can be dated from an event which took place on 28th October 1874.

Warfield Park was the home of Lord Ormathwaite and his wife, Lady Emily, daughter of the Duke of Beaufort. Lady Emily was a model of charity to the villagers, providing many of the services of to-day's Welfare State, and she was deservedly popular with them. There was therefore great ill-feeling against Lord Ormathwaite when, according to local gossip, he was said to be ill-treating his wife. So it was that the villagers *en masse* decided to show their sympathy for Lady Emily and disapproval of her husband by a demonstration of 'tin-canning'. Anything that could make a noise was used, including saucepans, drums, pails and whistles, as four hundred villagers marched in a ragged procession up the long drive to the house, banging away, shouting and singing.

Lord Ormathwaite was furious and came storming out of the house, ordering them to return instantly to their homes and noting the names of some of the ringleaders, who were duly summoned for unlawful assembly.

To-day, Warfield Park is no more and the Ormathwaites have gone, but a ghostly rabble is said to have been heard traipsing through the lanes during the autumn evenings, shouting and clashing their way to Warfield Park along a road which no longer exists.

WINDSOR

The town of Windsor probably has more stories of hauntings than the Castle, but as more and more houses are converted to offices and left empty at night, the stories about them for the most part date back some thirty or forty years.

Curfew House in Thames Street, across the road from the Curfew Tower, used to have a very sinister reputation. People visiting the house had the urge to throw themselves over the banisters, and one room was so haunted that the father-in-law of a young couple who lived there refused ever to sleep in the house again.

Two adjacent houses lower down Thames Street are both haunted, a fact which is perhaps not surprising considering that they must be at least four hundred years old. There is a tradition that they formed part of an inn, used in Tudor times to house the servants of guests at the Castle. In one of these houses, now a shop, two assistants have each felt a slight push in the back, as if a customer had bumped into them. In each instance this occurred in the same part of the building.

The house next door used to be owned by a very well-known Windsor family called Deacon, who moved there in 1916. One of the late Mr. Deacon's daughters has been kind enough to tell me of their experiences and to allow me to quote her mother's descrip-tions of what occurred. Early in their tenure of the house Mrs. Deacon disliked the atmosphere. 'I began to have very vivid dreams or visions', she wrote, 'when I always seemed to be fighting something evil, which never manifested itself in any shape but just as a thick black musty-smelling vapour. Whenever it appeared it formed a barrier which I could never pass beyond. Eventually some of the family began to complain of terrible nightmares of some horrible old man dragging off the bedclothes and trying to strangle them, and waking to find themselves bathed in perspiration and suffocating, the bedclothes all disarranged, as if they had been struggling with a real person. This went on for some time.' Mrs. Deacon, who was very psychic, was convinced that the root of the trouble lay somewhere down below. It was quite a while before the family discovered the cellar beneath the house, and they were amazed to find that it must have been used as a chapel at some period. Mrs. Deacon pointed unerringly to a part of the brick floor and asked one of her sons to start digging. This he did, only to uncover a medieval cooking pot (later displayed in the Guildhall Museum). But the pot was filled with the charred bones of babies. A Catholic priest was called in: he said prayers in the cellar and buried the bones in consecrated ground. This was the end of that particulr haunting.

Mrs. Deacon had other experiences, the most significant of which were her visions of Cardinal Wolsey. 'It was Easter week about 1921 or 1922, as far as I can ascertain', she wrote. 'I was not very well so I prepared a meal for the children for when they came home from school and went and lay down in my bedroom, which is a very quaint old room (Tudor). The room was *not* darkened as it was a bright spring morning, about noon. Something drew my attention to the opposite side of the room from where I was lying, and to my amazement I saw a figure, perfectly clearly. I knew at once it was Cardinal Wolsey, tall, well built, attired in the well-known red robe and hat. His face was not so clear as the whole figure but I knew at once instinctively that it was Cardinal Wolsey. There was no shadow of doubt in my mind, which was perfectly clear. He walked very slowly with bowed head, as if in deep thought. Slowly he passed right through my bed, through the wall, backwards and forwards, never looking to either side.

After pacing thus for about the fourth time the figure slowly dispersed before my eyes.

'I had gazed at him earnestly all the time, wondering what could be the cause of his appearing in that manner in this room and house, as I had never associated him with the house at any time. I was not a bit frightened, only perfectly mystified. Very soon after, my son, who was about 13 or 14, came to my room to enquire if there was anything which he could get for me. At once I asked him: did he know what became of Cardinal Wolsey when he was sent away from the Castle in disgrace by King Henry VIII? At once he replied: "He took refuge in an old inn in the town". Instantly I felt in my mind that this was the old inn. This was the first appearance.

'The second appearance was about two years after this, the first occurrence. Everything was the same (a peculiar coincidence), it being Holy Thursday noon. I was lying quietly resting, absolutely normal, the room in just the same condition and not darkened, when to my intense astonishment there appeared in exactly the same place Cardinal Wolsey, only in a black robe and head-dress. He was evidently in deep distress, wringing his hands together, his head bent down, and seemed old and worn. Without glancing at me or look-ing anywhere but absolutely straight in front of him, again he passed backwards and forwards through my massive mahogany bed, through the wall, continuing for about four to six times, then disappearing as mysteriously as he had appeared. The feeling it aroused in me was of pity and sympathy.'

I feel privileged to be allowed to publish Mrs. Deacon's account, as I had heard rumours of this story many years ago.

But the Deacons had another ghost, known to all the family as Fred. He was an old monk or priest in a brown cowl, and always seemed to be searching for something. He was a friendly ghost, and he may have regretted the departure of the Deacons after many years, as the present occupants of the building do not like using the upper part for fear of what they may see or hear.

At the foot of Thames Street, near the river, stands the Old

House Hotel, which is certainly haunted, but visitors to-day are unlikely to be disturbed by psychic occurrences except in one room. Although there is no proof that Sir Christopher Wren either built or occupied the house, the building is one of Windsor's finest specimens of early 18th century architecture. Very little is known about the house, but in the late 18th century it appears to have been owned by a prosperous coal merchant called Moore. Finding it too grand for his more modest requirements, Mr. Moore built another house nearby and let the main house to a series of tenants.

Earlier owners were a family called Cheshire, and they seem to have suffered various misfortunes: the eldest daughter's romance with a future peer was broken off, and the second daughter had a breakdown after having an illegitimate child which died in infancy. She never came out, but was reputed to take the air either in the early morning or at dusk. Finally, after nearly dying from food poisoning, Mr. Cheshire lost most of his money and the family had to move to more modest quarters. Over a century later the house was still being let, one frequent tenant being Baroness Vaux who used to take it for the summer months. Her London servants would refuse to stay, claiming that the house was haunted, and they had to be replaced by local labour, less susceptible to the occult.

Having been unoccupied for some years – sufficient in itself to give any building a bad reputation – the house was finally bought by two sisters, the Misses Outlaw, who ran it as a teashop and then as an hotel. According to a lady, whose father knew the sisters, the surviving Miss Outlaw was convinced that the house was haunted, and I have heard from other sources that the haunting was confined to one particular bedroom. This was confirmed for me by Mrs. Olive Eccles, who now lives in Windsor. Before moving to Windsor Mrs. Eccles and her husband stayed twice at the Old House Hotel, once in a large bedroom and on the second occasion in a much smaller room, reached by a back staircase. 'The thought of it being haunted', wrote Mrs. Eccles, 'had not crossed my mind, neither had I heard of a ghost connected with the house. One night we returned to the hotel about 12.45 a.m. after spending the evening with friends. We went straight to bed and fell asleep almost immediately. I awoke a little time later to see what I thought was a man standing in the darkened room by a chest of drawers. At first, I thought my husband must have got out of bed, but then realised it was too tall for him. I thought it must be a burglar and decided to keep very still to avoid possible attack and then to raise the alarm when he left the room. The figure then silently moved towards the bed. The bathroom door was opposite my head. When the figure reached the closed bathroom door, it vanished. I was fully awake. There were no shapes from shadows and the curtains were perfectly still. There was nothing menacing or frightening about the figure.'

My family moved to Windsor in 1930 and our first house, Ann Foord's House in Park Street, was certainly haunted. Although dating from the late 18th century, the house was built on much older foundations, which may possibly explain the nature of its ghost – a monk. The Eliot family from whom we leased the house knew him familiarly as 'Thomas' and he had been seen both by their children and their nurse, always in the upper part of the house and on the staircase.

'Thomas' never appeared to us, but sometimes at night when the top floor of the house was empty, we used to hear the sound of what seemed like heavy objects being moved about. There was also the curious phenomenon in one of the bedrooms of the sound of a little bell. This used to be heard early in the morning and seemed to indicate the first of the lesser hours – or Prime – in the Roman breviary. Looking back on the three years which we spent in that house, I recall a feeling of being watched, which was at times rather unnerving, and we were too cowardly to investigate the empty attics.

Quite recently, I heard an interesting story connected not with the house but with an object in it. The owner, the late Colonel Philip Eliot, had bought an old gun which he kept in his downstairs study. He knew nothing of its history. One day he showed it to a friend, who was obviously psychic as he declared that there was a misty figure standing nearby. He described it as having 'a sort of white handkerchief' over its head and neck. Colonel Eliot saw nothing. He later discovered that the gun was of a type used in the Foreign Legion.

I can speak with more authority about our next home in Windsor, 18th century Hadleigh House in Sheet Street, where we lived for nearly twenty-five years. One room had an unwelcoming feeling, nothing more, but the atmosphere of the house was generally friendly. Footsteps on the stairs at night were commonplace, but two incidents in particular stick in my mind. My mother had very catholic tastes in reading and was interested in many subjects, including the occult. In one book about what she laughingly called 'spookery', she read how an empty room had apparently been locked from the inside by occult forces and, as she read this, the thought passed through her mind that, while she could believe a lot of what was written in this particular book, the incident of the locked room seemed a bit far-fetched. The next morning, on coming downstairs to open up the house, we found that the drawing-room door would not open. The room was shuttered, as was the door at the back leading into the garden, and all the shutters were intact. One of the shutters was opened with considerable difficulty by a carpenter whom we summoned, and he found that a little bolt on the *inside* of the main door had been rammed in hard. This extraordinary phenomenon never happened again, but we felt that 'something' had picked up my mother's sceptical thoughts and had decided to teach her a lesson! Or was this a case of a poltergeist phenomenon, unconsciously generated by my mother?

Years passed. A number of spiritualist séances were held from time to time while we were there but nothing of importance occurred. Personally, I am not in favour of 'tampering with the unknown' in this manner and I seldom took part, and the room with its unfriendly feeling kept its secrets. It was in quite another part of the house that my mother and I shared a strange and wholly pleasant experience. One winter's evening, when the shutters had been closed and the curtains drawn, we were sitting in the dining-room eating supper. While speaking of everyday matters we were suddenly interrupted by loud knockings all round the room. We stopped talking only to find the room filled with the unmistakable scent of clove carnations. Needless to say, there were none in the house, and the phenomenon lasted about a minute.

About fifteen years later, many years after we had sold the house, the same phenomenon occurred in another part of the building. On this occasion the recipient was the daily help, who knew nothing of the story, and who summoned the mistress of the house to come and investigate. Curiously, she could smell nothing although her 'daily' insisted that the scent of clove carnations was all around her.

On the subject of séances, my mother did have one very interesting experience during World War II, when attending a spiritualist meeting in Windsor. On the whole she was extremely sceptical, but boredom in wartime, as much as anything else, persuaded her to participate. I was abroad in the Army and she wrote me an account of what happened. The medium was controlled for a long time by 'Goldilocks, a nasty little infant spirit, who laughs shrilly and talks in a high, childish voice - most precocious'. But much more interesting was the case of the Military Knight of Windsor, who 'came through'. He had died quite recently. 'The description of him was so good', she wrote, 'and the voice and manner so much like him, that I immediately recognised him as Colonel Egan. He said that he didn't know why no-one would speak to him now, as he was always seeing people in the streets whom he knew, so he was very glad that he could talk to us. He can't realise that he is dead.'

Tucked away behind the High Street there is a little house which used to be known as 'Anne Page's Cottage'. To-day it is used as a storeroom, but during World War II it was occupied by a Mrs. Tapley and her daughter. My mother wrote to me that she had visited them, as they had a room to let and she was always being asked to find accommodation for friends who wished to leave London. 'It's rather sweet', she wrote, 'smells old and musty and has a decided atmosphere. There is a dear little panelled sitting-room which is very haunted, with rustling skirts and a hostile ghost. Upstairs there is a more pleasant one.' Unfortunately, none of our friends wanted the spare room so I have no more information about the house.

My mother had one experience at Hadleigh House which, while not in any way ghostly, can definitely be described as paranormal. The incident was quite trivial but it seems to illustrate the argument propounded by Dunne in his *Experiment with Time*: that time, as we know it, is a man-made convenience, divided into past, present and future, and that 'real time' covers all three. I do not pretend to understand the theory, but it can certainly be put forward as an explanation of precognition of future events, as well, of course, as of many ghostly manifestations.

The incident took place soon after the end of World War II, when a casual acquaintance in London wrote to ask my mother to make friends with a Mrs. Preston who had taken a small house on an estate at Eton Wick, a few miles away. My mother had never been to Eton Wick and knew no-one living there, so she wrote to Mrs. Preston inviting her to tea one day. Mrs. Preston accepted.

On the night before the tea-party my mother dreamed of Mrs. Preston's visit. In the dream she took Mrs. Preston into the garden after tea, and asked her how she liked living at Eton Wick. Mrs. Preston replied that it was rather lonely as she knew no-one there, but that there was one unexpected advantage, the presence of an Italian dressmaker living a few doors away, who was able to alter all her clothes for her. This was soon after the war, when clothes rationing was still in force and make and mend was the order of the day.

Mrs. Preston duly came to tea. My mother did not recognise her as the person in her dream, but after tea she invited her to see the garden and asked her about life at Eton Wick. Mrs. Preston replied in the exact words that my mother had heard in her dream the previous night.

Friends of ours, John and Margaret Mills, bought a house lower down Sheet Street – number 29 – which they claimed was haunted. It had previously been a small private hotel and had then been occupied by a family who appear to have been undisturbed by anything unusual. But according to the Mills', an old man in a cloak haunted the stairs, and every morning objects on a shelf were re-arranged, and hats which had been hung on pegs were found on the floor. The house has now been turned into offices and is left unoccupied at night, leaving the ghostly visitant to his own devices.

Strange happenings, attributed to the supernatural, can, of course, often have a perfectly ordinary explanation. Take, for example, a case which I noted when undertaking research for my book on Windsor in Victorian times: in 1841 members of a family called Wright, living at Clewer, were so terrified by loud knockings and explosions, audible a hundred yards away, that they left their house, and the affair aroused such public interest that the local magistrates, accompanied by two un-named 'scientific gentlemen from Newbury', decided to investigate. The noises, which by that time had ceased, had clearly come from the earth-closet which was, of course, the only form of sanitation in those days. The opinion of the investigators was that the disturbances were caused by the explosion of 'noxious gases' rather than by the supernatural, and the Wright family were presumably advised to have their privy emptied and cleaned in order to avoid further trouble.

But I have no doubts at all about other very strange occurrences in another house in Sheet Street. Old Institute House is basically 18th century, but with older features incorporated in it, and my informant was a very level-headed man, Mr. Frederick Bentley, who had a top floor flat in the building. Mr. Bentley is a former C.I.D. officer and in the course of his duties he was often called out late at night by the local police. On a number of occasions, when returning home in the early hours of the morning he would be conscious of a remarkable drop in temperature on reaching the landing on the first floor. Another person, too, had remarked on the eeriness of this particular part of the house, but this was nothing to Mr. Bentley's experience one night when he was alone in his flat. Having followed his usual custom of reading until he was ready for sleep, Mr. Bentley switched off the light. There was a bay window on the south side overlooking a flat roof, and on the east side a small leaded pane window faced the garden. The moon shone brilliantly through the little window.

Mr. Bentley was suddenly conscious that he was not alone in the room, although there was no sound of breathing. Sitting up in bed, he saw a figure. Let Mr. Bentley describe it in his own words. 'He could not have been more than five feet six inches in height, was beautifully proportioned and may well have been stark naked! In my sitting position in bed, I was unable to see his lower limbs, but his head, arms and torso were perfectly visible. He was standing at a slight angle, which permitted the moon partially to illuminate his body. My action was almost automatic after my first reaction of utter disbelief. Turning a little I shouted, "What the hell do you think you're doing?" As I said it I rolled sideways and switched on the bedside lamp. The room was flooded with light but the intruder had gone.'

Mr. Bentley searched the room and it was quite obvious to him that no-one was in it and that nobody could have gone out through either window. He realised that there could only be one explanation – he had seen a ghost.

'I can see my visitor even now', said Mr. Bentley. 'He was a native of some kind, possibly a Polynesian, for his skin was lighter than that of most coloured men and his hair, which was thick and crinkly, was rather short, but appeared rounded as if indicative of the shape of his head. His body glistened and gave me the impression that it was coated with oil of some description. But it was his eyes! His eyes were extremely large and wide open, the whites seeming to increase the size of them. He just stood there staring at me, his expression seeming to be one of curiosity. There was nothing menacing about him or his attitude. Only after I had switched on the light and completed my search of the room did I begin to feel a little uneasy. If you have seen a dog's hackles rise as it confronts another dog and prepares to fight, this is precisely what I felt. I could actually feel the hair standing on the back of my neck.'

Mr. Bentley's theory is that he saw the ghost of a member of the leper colony, housed in the pest house at the bottom of Sheet Street. I am doubtful of this explanation for two reasons: first, the leper colony was at Spital, not in Sheet Street, and the pest house, later the town's workhouse and then the gaol, was on the opposite side of the road, beyond the site of the Victoria Barracks. But Mr. Bentley is undoubtedly psychic and I am sure that whatever he saw can be classified as paranormal, possibly even the wraith of a living person.

As an enthusiastic gardener Mr. Bentley cultivated a piece of land behind his house, possibly part of the extensive grounds of Abbey House which was demolished to make way for the present administrative offices of the Royal Borough of Windsor and Maidenhead. One Sunday evening he had been mowing his lawn when he had a feeling that he was being watched. Again, I must let Mr. Bentley tell the story in his own words. 'I had my back to the area which previously had been Abbey House and its grounds. Some fifteen or twenty yards away I could see vaguely a number of figures. They were indistinct and what I could see of their clothing was mainly long cloaks or gowns, but one thing was reasonably distinct and significant – the figure on the extreme right of the line was wearing a tall hat with a wide brim and a white sort of collar of unusual size. I just stood and stared, but had no urge to investigate. It was a warm night but I suddenly felt chilled. Later that night I realised where I had seen such a tall hat and white collar – this was the traditional dress of the Puritans of Cromwell's period.'

Mr. Bentley is convinced that excavations on the site of the grounds of Abbey House may reveal much of interest.

There seems no rational explanation for a story about Park Street which has all the hallmarks of a traditional haunting. Leading off the street is a passage way, known as Black Horse Yard, the only reminder of an old inn of that name which used to be there. Many of the 18th century houses in the street have now been turned into offices and this applies to Gate House, near Black Horse Yard. For many years the house belonged to a Miss Smith, who had lived there with her aunt, and the family were firm believers in the story that the house was haunted but that manifestations only occurred just before the death of the reigning Sovereign. According to tradition, the haunting was that of a coach, leaving Black Horse Yard and conveying one of the royal physicians to the bedside of Charles II as he lay dying. I heard the story from a niece of Miss Smith and she wrote it down for me. 'Just before the death of Edward VII', she wrote, 'both my aunt and her own aunt and two maids heard a great deal of noise in the cellar. She said it was just like furniture being moved about. They all spoke to each other about it and said they could not sleep well because of it, and then the papers announced the sudden illness of the King.' I do not know if any manifestations have been seen or heard at the time of the deaths of subsequent Sovereigns.

Another house in the town reputed to be haunted was Long Walk House, in King's Road. The older part, at the back, was supposed to be haunted by a woman – no other details have survived – and the house had the reputation of being unlucky for its occupants. After being used for some years as a Y.W.C.A. hostel the building was demolished and a new hostel built near the site.

The former Travers College in Datchet Road is a graceful building, dating from 1803, when it was founded as a home for indigent naval officers, known as Naval Knights. The six Knights and their Governor had separate dwelling-houses with a communal dining-room, and it is one of the Governors, an Admiral, who is said to haunt the building. The Naval Knights seem never to have been happy with their lot and the charitable scheme was abandoned in 1892, but the last Governor was reluctant to leave, and it is supposed to be his ghost that haunts the place. The building is now a boys school for the choristers of St. George's Chapel.

The Theatre Royal is an Edwardian building, replacing an early 19th century theatre which was totally destroyed in a disastrous fire in 1908. Not only was the theatre burnt out but a girl, called Charlotte, was burnt to death, and her ghost is said to haunt the building which replaced the one in which she met her death.

How does one account for the sudden drops in temperature which so often accompany paranormal phenomena? The 16th century Elizabethan House in Peascod Street is haunted by footsteps going upstairs, but never down. The owner of the shop, her husband and their assistant have all heard the footsteps and felt the sudden chill.

Knowing of my interest in the paranormal, Mrs. Patricia Griffith, when working for Itek International, drew my attention to the ghostly happenings in their headquarters office building, then situated in No. 1 Thames Street. It was in 1811 that an Eton confectioner, Charles Layton, moved into these premises, and his business was to thrive in his family for well over a century, until the premises were taken over by the firm of Findlater, Mackie & Todd. Before the time of Charles Layton, the building had undoubtedly been an inn or lodging house. When, in 1897, extensions were being made to the adjoining Great Western Railway Station, a lead coffin, containing a body wearing a woollen cap and shroud, was discovered. It was generally assumed that this was the body of a Hawaiian chieftain, one of a group who had visited George III.

During the Findlater tenure of the building, when the manager and his wife lived on the premises, ghostly manifestations were first recorded. Mrs. Baldrey, the manager's wife, gave me the details. She was in the upstairs flat alone when she saw a figure coming towards her – 'like someone in a cap and gown, and male', she described it. Some months later she woke in the middle of the night to see a tall, well-built man in a straw hat. He turned, went out and closed the bedroom door, something which she and her husband never did. A few months later, the same figure appeared in the bedroom. He seemed to smile at Mrs. Baldrey, raised his hat, walked to the door, turned, nodded and smiled again. She had the feeling that he had departed for good and she never saw him again.

The Baldreys also heard ghostly footsteps and their dog would growl and bare his teeth, something which they never knew him to do. These footsteps continued when the building was taken over by Itek International. In fact, early morning cleaners imagined that there must be burglars on the premises as they knew that officially it was empty. The figure described as wearing a cap and gown, or a coachman's cloak with a cape on top, was also seen by members of the staff. Mrs. Griffith wrote to me: 'I am quite convinced that alongside the every-day business of Itek International there is another 'period of time' in existence. I think that the sightings we see are persons in another plane of time-zone, going about their daily lives.'

Whatever the explanation for ghostly footsteps, they can be very unnerving. A lady told me of an experience she had had in the 1920s, in the days when Gilbert & Sullivan operas used to be performed in the now demolished Albert Institute. The principal organiser was a Mr. Webb, a local butcher, who lived in Vansittart Road, Windsor. This lady, then a young woman, had to call at the house one day in connection with a forthcoming production. As she was sitting talking to Mr. and Mrs. Webb there was a knock at the front door, but the Webbs took no notice. The knocking was repeated twice before my informant broke off what she was saying to remark that there was someone at the door. Mrs. Webb replied that there was no-one there and there was nothing to worry about. Later on, Mrs. Webb told her that the house was haunted, that they frequently heard these knockings, and that they often heard footsteps on the stairs at night. However, they had learnt to live with these phenomena.

Trinity Place is very much older than Vansittart Road, and I was told by a lady who had lived there that on one occasion she had felt a heavy hand on her shoulder when she was in bed. This only happened once, but she was told by a friend that the house had been the scene of a murder in World War II, when a woman had been strangled.

Another local resident recalled how her father, cigar in hand, would always open the kitchen door at a quarter past six and ask:

'Is dinner ready yet?' After his death, on several occasions when she was in the kitchen she would smell cigar smoke, always at 6.15 p.m. A friend who was staying in the house once commented that she was surprised at her smoking cigars. My informant told her that she did not, and asked her friend what time it was when she had smelt cigar smoke. Not surprisingly, she replied: 'About a quarter past six.'

A late Georgian house in Gloucester Place, which used to belong to friends of mine, John and Phoebe Mumford, appeared to have had a ghost in the garden. One day in brilliant sunshine my friend was working in the garden when a man, dressed in grey, in the style of the 1920s, and wearing a cap or hat, approached her and disappeared three or four feet away. The tinkle of bells was sometimes heard in the house.

Gloucester Place has always struck me as a peaceful spot, so I was all the more surprised to hear from a correspondent that a friend had felt constrained to move from there, because of a great feeling of evil, not so much in the houses, but in the road, particularly at the far end. Several people had independently vouched for having had the same experience, and had moved away.

Two men were emphatic that they must have hit a woman as they drove along St. Leonards Road towards the King Edward VII Hospital. They saw her suddenly appear in front of their car but they felt no bump. The driver immediately stopped but there was no sign of anyone.

The old operating theatre – now disused – at the Hospital is said to be haunted by the ghost of the surgeon, Sir Joseph Skeffington, who lived in Osborne Road, and several houses in Windsor, used as nurses' quarters, were thought to be haunted. These included Castle Hill House and a house in Frances Road but details of paranormal happenings are lacking.

The Engine House Restaurant in Church Lane, near the Guildhall, is haunted. One of the staff recently reported seeing a ghostly figure. 'He wore a stiff white collar', she said, 'a hat like a Quaker, had long flowing hair and a beard – and then disappeared.'

Other staff have heard someone moving about upstairs. 'Some mornings the bath has large male footprints in it but there are no men living here.' So reported the manageress to the *Windsor and Eton Express*.

One of the most tantalising Windsor hauntings used to take place in a cinema which has now been pulled down. As a schoolboy, some fifty-odd years ago, I remember the Playhouse Cinema being built on the site of some 18th century houses, the ground floor of one of which had been turned into a bicycle shop. Over the years, numerous members of the staff in the cinema had paranormal experiences: the sight of a woman in a long dress standing on the stage, the sound of running footsteps, and sudden drops in temperature. Occasionally, the manager's dog would be terrified and refuse to move. Many of these events occurred about mid-February, and one wonders if the hauntings will survive the second rebuilding. One theory which has been put forward is that the manifestations relate to an unsolved murder of a woman in the bicycle shop.

Another building which has recently been pulled down is the New British School, established in 1841 by a local philanthropist, Joseph Chariott. Before its demolition, part of the school was used as the Borough Education Office. Members of the staff used often to hear footsteps in the empty room above, perhaps those of Joseph Chariott or of some long-forgotten master who lived above the school.

WINDSOR CASTLE

The earliest reference to paranormal happenings in the Castle is to be found in Sir William Dugdale's *Historia*. According to Sir William, the ghost of George, Duke of Buckingham appeared on several occasions to his manservant, Parker, and to a former school friend called Towes. The latter was in the Castle one day in 1628 when he suddenly cried out: 'The Duke of Buckingham has been assassinated!' He later stated that it was Buckingham's ghost that had warned him. According to witnesses, Towes cried out at the very moment when the Duke was struck with a dagger by his assassin, Felton, at Portsmouth.

Windsor Castle, steeped in history and crammed with mementoes of the past, should, one would think, have a reputation for being haunted. Although there are many stories of ghostly apparitions, I have heard only one first-hand account. But first let us deal with the more important ghostly figures who are said to haunt the Castle. I have never found any confirmation of the story that the unfortu-nate Queen Anne Boleyn has been seen at a window in the Dean's Cloister. If the Deanery is haunted, the ghost is not that of King Charles I whose body, after execution, lay in its coffin overnight on a table – the table still there – before being hurriedly buried in the vaults beneath St. George's Chapel. The sound of ghostly footsteps going up four stairs has according to the author, Hector Bolitho, been heard in the Deanery, where modifications to the structure have left only three stairs, and I was told some forty years ago that a little boy had been seen standing in the door of a bedroom in one of the Canon's houses, then occupied by Canon Crawley. 'I don't want to go riding today', he said, and vanished.

There is a persistent legend that Queen Elizabeth I haunts the Royal Library, which in her own times formed the State Apartments. The story received considerable publicity in 1897, the year of Queen Victoria's Diamond Jubilee, when an account was published based on the experience of an Officer of the Guard, who availed himself of the privilege of visiting the Library while on duty. The story is worth quoting in full. Here it is:

'It is perhaps only a curious coincidence that, in this record year of Her Majesty's reign, the nephew of the last English bishop who did homage to Queen Victoria should have seen with his own eyes the ghost of Queen Elizabeth in the Library of Windsor Castle.

'The story, which appears to be as well authenticated as any records of the incidents of every day in the morning papers, tells how Lieutenant Glyn of the 3rd Battalion of the Grenadier Guards was sitting in Windsor Castle Library, reading *The History of Dorsetshire*, when he became aware of someone passing into the inner library. He looked up and saw a female figure in black with black lace on her head falling on to her shoulders. He was sitting in a chair on the east of the first room, from which a few steps led up into a gallery built by Queen Elizabeth as a picture gallery, and after traversing it so far turn sharply to the right and disappear into a bay, from where, in former times, the great Queen used to descend by a staircase to the Terrace. It was four o'clock on a February afternoon, just before closing time. When the attendant came to close the door, Lieutenant Glyn asked who was the lady who was at work in the inner room. "No-one", said the attendant. "But" said he, "I have just seen her now walk into the inner room". The attendant went to see, found no-one and returned. "She must have gone out of a door in that corner", said Mr. Glyn, pointing to the bay from which, in olden times, the gallery staircase ran down to the Terrace. "But there is no door there", said the attendant.

'Greatly marvelling at the sudden disappearance of the lady in black, the Lieutenant departed, little thinking that he had been the first man in the present reign to see the ghost of the famous Elizabeth. When the attendant reported the occurrence to the Librarian, Dr. Holmes, he at once sent for Mr. Glyn and asked for a description of the figure. When he had given it the Librarian said, "It is the same. You have seen the apparition of Queen Elizabeth."

'It seems that from old time Windsor Castle has been visited by the famous Queen from time to time. The Empress Frederick, when a child, is said to have seen the apparition in the same place. The Librarian has been familiar with the story for twenty-seven years, and often at Hallowe'en has sat late waiting to see the ghost, but in vain.' So much for the account, which was published in 1897.

There seems no reason to doubt that the young lieutenant saw a ghost, but the automatic identification with Queen Elizabeth puzzles me. First, Mr. Glyn did not himself recognise the Queen's unmistakable appearance – haughty manner, flaming red wig, distinctive profile, gorgeous dress and jewels. This identification was automatically made by the Librarian, Dr. Holmes, who declared that he himself had heard the story soon after his appointment in 1870. Nearly three hundred years had passed since the death of the Queen, so numerous people would have used the rooms during this period. Any one of them might have left a ghostly imprint behind. Sir Owen Morshead, who was for many years the Royal Librarian, first told me the story in outline but I have only recently come across the complete narrative. As far as I know, the Royal Library has remained ghost-free for the last eighty odd years.

Finally, the story that Queen Victoria's eldest daughter, the Empress Frederick, who, when a child, is said to have seen a ghost in the Library, does not appear ever to have been recorded at the time. It presumably rests on the word of Dr. Holmes who, of course, became Librarian many years after the Princess had grown up and married, and who was so quick to identify the ghost seen by Mr. Glyn with that of Queen Elizabeth.

In his erudite book on Windsor Castle Sir Owen tells another story, which seems to be well authenticated, about the ghost of George III who, during the last years of his life, was confined to a set of rooms below the Royal Library. To all intents and purposes the King was mad.

The King's gloomy rooms overlooked the North Terrace, and in his saner moments, on hearing the approach of the guard, the King would stand at the window to see them pass below and would raise his right hand in acknowledgment of the Guard Commander's 'Eyes Right'. The King died there on 29th January 1820, and his body, in its coffin, lay in state in another part of the Castle while preparations went ahead for the funeral. The routine of changing the various posts went on as usual, and as the Ensign passed the old King's rooms he automatically looked up and, to his surprise, saw the bearded figure that he knew so well. The well trained Guards followed his command 'Eyes Right', and the figure made the customary response.

What makes the story especially interesting is that the young officer was William Knollys, who many years later was to be made Comptroller to the young Prince of Wales, later Edward VII. Sir William, as he became, lived to a great age, and he told the story to the Prince's second son who was to become George V.

There are, of course, many well authenticated stories of people, at the moment of death, being seen somewhere else – I consider this to be a form of telepathy – but the appearance of a person some days after death is a different matter.

So much for the royal ghosts. Talk to any guardsman who has been on sentry duty in the Castle during the hours of darkness and one will soon learn that certain posts are most unpopular.

Two elderly ladies told me a story which had been passed down from an earlier generation, so the incident may have happened in the 19th century. One evening, a Guardsman on duty on the East Terrace saw an extraordinary creature which he described as being like an elephant. He was so frightened that he shot at it. The bullet passed through the animal, chipping the castle wall. The creature vanished. The same ladies spoke of the ghost of a little woman in a brown dress who appeared where part of the royal archives were stored, but she was looked upon as a friend.

I mentioned earlier that I knew of only one first-hand account of a ghost in Windsor Castle. This was from a man who as a boy lived in one of the houses in the Horseshoe Cloisters. One day he was washing his hands at the kitchen sink when suddenly he saw a man, leading a horse, cross the room and vanish into the wall beyond. The maid of all work, who was also in the kitchen, saw this too, but neither of them was believed by the rest of the family. Some time later, however, when repairs were being undertaken in the kitchen, a large underground stable was found behind the wall into which the horse and groom had disappeared.

Several other houses in the Horseshoe Cloisters appear to be haunted. In one, occupied at the time by the Head Chorister and his family, the ghost of a woman in white used to appear every evening at 6 o'clock. The family looked on her as a friend, but more recently – whether or not in the same house I do not know – the occupants were so disturbed by 'something' that they asked to be moved.

The Mary Tudor Tower in the Lower Ward of the Castle seems to have a well established tradition of ghostly footsteps on the stairs. The late Miss Kavanagh, who lived there for many years with her parents, when her father, General Sir Charles Kavanagh, was Governor of the Military Knights, told me that she often heard footsteps coming up the stairs to her bedroom door at the top of the house. At first she thought that they must belong to the family's chauffeur but after he had left their employment the footsteps continued. She was once lent an old book about Windsor Castle and in this she read that an earlier inhabitant of the Tower had had precisely similar experiences.

Another strange phenomenon which used to worry overnight guests was a wall between two bedrooms which seemed to move. Possibly a trick of light, but who can tell?

Looking through some old letters of my mother's, I have come across an account, written in 1935, of a conversation she had with the widow of a former Governor of the Military Knights, Mrs. Carteret Carey. 'Mrs. Carteret Carey', she wrote, 'tells me that the house is haunted by that woman in a grey dress and white cap whom Lady Kavanagh saw. In their (Carteret Carey's) time they often saw her. She was a serving maid of Queen Elizabeth's time who had been very badly treated and had had an illegitimate baby. Princess Alice (Countess of Athlone) insisted on having a séance in the drawing-room and they found out that this had happened in the time of a Governor called de Burgh, and verified it in an old record.'

One building which is certainly haunted is the Norman Tower, adjoining the Round Tower. In spite of its rather gruesome history, one room, the so-called Prison Room, above the Norman

Gate, having been used as a prison during the Civil War, seems to be haunted by the harmless ghost of an elderly man. Children playing in the room have seen him and have not been at all frightened. Other people living in the Norman Tower have sensed someone brushing past them in one of the passages, but the atmosphere is perfectly happy and peaceful.

These are some of the ghosts of Windsor Castle. It would be surprising if there were not others in an edifice so steeped in history. Perhaps there are: I have, for instance, heard rumours of a haunting in a very private part of the Castle which has so frightened staff on duty late at night that they insist on working in pairs. This, at least, is what I was told by the late Mrs. Joan Hewitt, who in turn had heard the story from the wife of one of the royal footmen.

I have often been asked if I know anything of the story that Queen Victoria used to have séances with John Brown, and that the records had been destroyed by Dr. Randall Davidson, Dean of Windsor and later Archbishop of Canterbury. I have, of course, no information on the subject, except to have read the rumour that Brown was a medium. However, someone once told me that King George VI, rummaging in a drawer, had found one of these séance records hidden at the back, which Davidson must have overlooked. Whatever the truth of this story, Davidson certainly persuaded Queen Victoria to destroy the manuscript of the book about John Brown which she had written.

Finally, what about Herne the Hunter?

Anyone interested in pursuing the fascinating subject of the origins of the legend of the 'Wild Hunt' should read Mr. M. J. Petry's erudite book, *Herne the Hunter*, published in 1972. The legend dates from pre-Christian times and is widespread all over Europe. As to Herne himself, the stories of his haunting have been magnified out of all proportion by Harrison Ainsworth's novel *Windsor Castle*, which was first published in 1843 and is largely fiction.

We have to turn to Shakespeare's *Merry Wives of Windsor* for the first printed reference to Herne, and this is what he wrote:

There is an old tale goes, that Herne the hunter,
Sometime a keeper here in Windsor forest,
Doth all the winter-time, at still midnight,
Walk round about an oak, with ragged horns –
And there he blasts the tree, and takes the cattle,
And makes the milch-kine yield blood, and shakes a chain,

In a most hideous and dreadful manner ...
You have heard of such a spirit, and well you know
The supersitious idle-headed eld
Received, and did deliver to our age,
This tale of Herne the hunter for a truth.

There seems little doubt that the oak, known as Herne's Oak, stood in the Home Park and that in 1796, when it was in a decayed state, it was felled with a number of other dead and dying trees. An oak was planted on or near the real site in the reign of Edward VII, after another so-called Herne's Oak had been planted on the wrong site in Queen Victoria's time.

Samuel Ireland in 1793 and James Hakewell in 1813 took up the story, and the latter wrote: 'The traditional account is that Herne was a keeper in the forest at the time of Elizabeth and, having committed some offence, took the desperate solution to hang himself upon this oak.'

All subsequent accounts of Herne are based on these three authorities, and the story has been embroidered at will.

Has Herne ever been seen or heard? There are reports, unconfirmed, of course, that he appears beneath the oak at times of crisis in the nation's history. I have come across three accounts, which are worth considering.

The father of the present Lord Burton is reputed to have heard the baying of hounds and the huntsman's horn in Windsor Great Park, when he was a boy at Eton. As he was born in 1894 this must have occurred a few years before World War I. Unfortunately, he does not seem ever to have spoken of the affair to his son, or to have left a written record, so precise details as to time and place are lacking.

Another report was that of Mrs. Walter Legge, whom I

remember well before World War II when she was living at Old Windsor. She was a very sensible person and a Justice of the Peace. On two occasions, probably in 1926, she heard the baying of hounds at midnight, coming from the direction of the Great Park towards the Castle. The second time this happened she was joined by her daughter, who also heard the same sounds. Having for many years known Mrs. Legge's grandson, I asked him if he could throw any light on the story and, although he was a schoolboy at the time, he certainly remembered hearing about it. 'I well recall my grandmother and mother talking about it', he wrote. 'They were quite convinced that it was definitely not a 'tangible pack' as it was midnight or 1 a.m. when they heard it, having come back from London and were thus standing outside the house for a breath of air before going to bed. The run was, I gather, in the direction of Bears' Rails from the Copper Horse. Who knows?'

Who, indeed, knows what these ladies heard? Dogs chasing cats or rabbits? Although remaining at Old Windsor for many years, they never heard the midnight baying again.

In Count Nikolai Tolstoy's recently published *The Quest for Merlin*, he refers to a conversation which he once had with an old friend, the poet, Charles Richard Cammell. The latter told him that, when a boy at Eton before the Great War, he had frequently talked with an old keeper, who had seen Herne plunge by on his endless chase.

A more recent instance, immediately associated by the press with Herne, took place in September 1976 when a Guardsman, on sentry duty on the East Terrace, near the State Apartments, was found unconscious when his relief came. Later, the soldier told his officer that he had collapsed when one of the statues in the so-called Italian Garden became horned and came to life. This sentry post is a lonely one and it is, of course, possible that the young soldier's imagination was fired by the scudding clouds in the moonlight.

All we can say about the legend of Herne the Hunter is that the evidence for a specific haunting of a particular spot in Windsor Great Park or Forest is negligible. Any report of a ghostly rider or of phantom hounds seen or heard within a very wide area – that previously covered by Windsor Forest – is automatically attributed to Herne the Hunter, himself a shadowy figure at the best of times, and in my view most of these stories can be discounted. But, in the words of one authority, 'his ancestry goes back to Odin'.

The present Earl of Gowrie, who spent some years in the Castle as a child, takes the view that the legend of Herne is a survival of a fertility god of some kind. My own opinion is that there must have been forest shrines, guarded over by priests who, as part of their ritual, may have worn some form of antlered head-dress, and that Herne is a folk memory, handed down from our pre-Christian ancestors.

WINDSOR GREAT PARK

Earlier in this book I have referred to a haunted house at Caesar's Camp at Bracknell. The lady who told me of her experiences has never forgotten a summer evening's walk which she took with a boy-friend in the Park in the 1930s. At that time the Park was completely open and contained herds of deer. About nine o'clock that night, while the young couple were still walking, there was a sudden thunderstorm with torrential rain. There were then some long, covered racks near the A332 road from which the deer could get fodder and it was under one of these that the two young people took shelter. Suddenly the girl realised that there was a tall figure, dressed in a black cloak and wearing a tall black hat, standing by her. She made some remark about the weather, but he never spoke and turned his back. Both she and her friend suddenly felt terrified and, without speaking a word to one another, they fled from their shelter into the storm, convinced that their companion did not belong to this world.

In 1937 or 1938 at 11.30 in the morning probably the same figure was seen by a Mrs. Hill who was taking her small children for a walk in the Long Walk. About five minutes after they had passed through the gates half way up the avenue and were resting on the grass, Mrs. Hill saw the figure on the right hand side. 'I did not realise it was a ghost at first', she wrote to me. 'I saw the man a long distance off. I thought he was going to a party at Windsor Castle by the way he was dressed. He had a large brimmed hat on, a long black cape with collar turned up, and he was very tall. It was not until he reached a cluster of deer that I realised he was a ghost. He was gliding right through them. The deer just turned their heads in his direction but did not move. When I saw the ghost gliding through the deer I just got hold of my children and hugged them to me. I was too terrified to get up. The perspiration was pouring down my face – it looked as though he was heading for us. When he was about five feet away he swiftly turned and went to the side of a large tree about six feet away.'

Mrs. Hill could see his eyes – very dark brown or black – under the brim of his hat. He had, she said, rather a long face and a straight nose.

WINKFIELD

Once a house has the reputation of being haunted, the fact is often remembered long after it has changed hands any number of times. This used to be more of a problem than it is to-day, as resident staff would refuse to stay. Nowadays, in these servantless times, the owners must look after their houses as well as cope with the ghosts.

A house behind Drift Road in Winkfield, called Nobbscrook

Farm, used to be the home of a Mrs. Drury-Lowe. A correspondent has written to me about the haunting there. 'I remember', she wrote, 'my mother's friend – who was a companion to Mrs. Drury-Lowe – saying that it was impossible to keep any domestic staff because of a woman in a mob cap who used to walk the corridors at night. There was a pond at the side of the house which none of Mrs. Drury-Lowe's horses would pass after dusk'. Whether the two aspects of the paranormal were connected, one does not know.

To-day, forty years later, the house is apparently peaceful enough, although to some people it has the feeling of being haunted by a friendly ghost.

Another house in Drift Road, called Orchard Lea, is supposed to have been the setting for a fight between two brothers, one of whom was drowned in a lake in the grounds. To this day, people refuse to sleep in the bedrooms on the top floor, but the connection between the top floor and the lake seems rather far-fetched.

Before moving to Ascot we used to live in a late Victorian house at Cranbourne, formerly part of Winkfield. The atmosphere of the house was very peaceful, and only one rather strange incident occurred there during our five year tenure. One day, when my wife was alone in the house, she was standing in the kitchen near the open door which led into a passage. Suddenly the atmosphere became intensely cold and she had the impression – nothing more – that someone had passed down the passage. There was, of course, nobody there, and the kitchen immediately regained its normal temperature.

New Lodge, a large Victorian battlemented mansion, has seen many changes of use since it was the home of its builder, Baron van de Weyer, whose daughter married the second Lord Esher. His ghost – or at least that of an elderly man – appears to have been seen on several occasions, dressed in old-fashioned clothes. Sometimes the figure was quite clear, at other times rather hazy. Outside the house, a man on a motorcycle recently had a strange experience. Riding down Drift Road towards New

Lodge, he saw a coach, drawn by white horses, suddenly dash out of the drive and across the road, where it disappeared up what is now a disused road.

WOKINGHAM

Several books on ghosts and hauntings refer to the Old Rose Inn as being haunted, the ghostly figure supposed to be that of a girl who was jilted by her lover and hanged herself in one of the bedrooms. The original inn, however, was demolished, and it is now the site of the Co-operative Supermarket. The new inn has no history of being haunted.

YATTENDON

There is an amusing story about the daughter of a former vicar who is said to have haunted the Vicarage at one time: an attractive ghost in a grey dress. No-one was frightened of her and she herself obviously enjoyed social occasions and parties, appearing in the kitchen when preparations were being made. But the haunting seems to have ceased and she has not been seen for some years. Possibly the scale of entertaining to-day is too modest to attract her.

APPENDIX

AN ASCOT POLTERGEIST

I am indebted to the owners for permission to print this account of the strange happenings in their house in Fernbank Road, which covered the period Christmas 1974 until early in 1976.

Nothing out of the ordinary occurred on the one occasion when I visited the house, and spoke to the owners about their experiences, and there was nothing 'spooky' about the house, quite to the contrary, as it was a modern well-built building, light and airy, furnished in contemporary style, and all the family were obviously very level-headed. The story has not been edited in any way by me.

In a covering letter, Mrs. —— states: 'I must say we all missed the phenomena when they stopped happening. It was all very exciting and it was like having an old friend at the house as it continued for so many months'. Here is her account:

'We moved into this house in June 1973. All was normal until around Christmas 1974 when the boys began telling us that they had noticed flashes of light outside their bedroom windows (they have a room each on opposite sides of the house). We took no notice of this until in the early spring of 1975, we too began to notice brilliant flashes of light outside our house. They appeared in both the back and front gardens – during the day or evening. Sometimes they would start at the week-ends soon after breakfast and would still be occurring when we went to bed. None of the neighbours commented on them so we presumed they hadn't seen them, although we asked.

Then my next door neighbour was talking to me over the fence one Sunday afternoon and she saw a really vivid flash down the centre of my kitchen, the door which was open and facing him. Another neighbour to whom we had given a lift late one night and who had also been told about the flashes, was about to walk out of our gate at about 11.30 p.m. having been waiting about for a few minutews to see whether the flashes would occur, when there was suddenly a brilliant blue flash off the chimney pot. (I should mention that we had called in the Electricity Board around March and described the flashes, but they could find no fault at all in the overhead power supply to the house and were unable to produce the flashes.) One sunny evening we stood at the front window actually watching a beam of light like a neon tube running backwards and forwards from the bumper of my VW car to the wooden garage door and then appearing to come from the hub caps too.

The flashes began to come inside the house in late spring. We could actually hear the pop when the occurred close to us. They had the ability to appear in all the rooms at the same time by coming under the doors – that is to say, when we were in our separate bedrooms or the bathroom we could all see them bouncing under the doors. They became so frequent that we called in Professor John Taylor of King's College who, although he promised to watch them several times, was unable to come down. By this time static electricity had been discounted. If we were sitting in the garden on a sunny day, the flashes would just be going off all around us, one after the other, for the whole day.

During this time there were several other phenomena which we didn't then associate with the flashes. For instance, on two days on succession, the bulbs and shades of the wall lights on either side of the fireplace suddenly jumped out of their sockets. Then my younger son mislaid his Timex watch one Friday. After scouring the house for it we decided on Sunday that he must have left it at school, when my eye was caught by something gleaming on one of the wall lights. I was staggered on closer inspection, to see that my son's watch had been tightly strapped to the black wrought iron with its face to the wall, and if it hadn't been for the sun glinting on the buckle, it could have been there unnoticed for weeks. The really amazing thing, however, was the fact that this cheap watch, which runs for about 30 hours only without winding, was fully wound and absolutely correct!

Another odd thing which around this time, was the moving door mat. One Saturday night in April 1975 we had a late party and by the time I had cleared up and got up to bed, it was about 2.30 in the morning. Although I was the last up to bed, we were going to the 8 o'clock church service and so I was also the first up. To my astonishment the coconut mat from the front door had been neatly positioned halfway up our staircase. Everyone disclaimed responsibility and I accepted their disclaimers, because it was such a futile thing for anyone to do. The doormat episode was repeated once more before I realised it was part of the happenings.

All through the summer the brilliant flashes continued inside and out. I remember on one particular occasion my husband was sitting on the stairs making a call overseas and the flashes were going off with loud pops over his head every few seconds. Around this time we began to realise that 'it' (whatever it was) was able to listen in on the telephone wires. So many people had heard of our happenings they always asked about them when they rang us. And we realised that each time 'it' was mentioned, there was loud interference on the line. My husband actually tested it on several occasions when there was someone who knew about it listening at the other end. He would ask 'it' to buzz twice if it was listening and we never failed to get double buzz. A number of people will confirm that when 'it' was discussed, the intereference on the line was so bad that we could hardly hear each other.

Also in the summer we had the episode of the flower pots. I was washing up one evening at the sink, which is under a window overlooking the garden, when suddenly something struck the wall just below the window. When I went out, I saw it was an empty plastic flower pot. Now plastic flower pots are so light that it is impossible to throw them any distance – we've tried! After that, flower pots were thrown with monotonous regularity at the French windows of the sitting room – usually in the dark. There is no way any one of our neighbours could throw them in that direction, since the fence at that side borders a stream and we had positive proof of this one particular evening.

We had been watching television and it was dark, 9 o'clock exactly. There was a smack on the glass which made us all jump out of jour skins and we pulled back the curtains and saw in the reflected light from the room, a flower pot rolling around. I know this sounds impossible, but we let the curtains fall back and my husband went out to pick up the pot and it had disappeared! He called us all out to look. The pot had been rolling around on a terrace which is bordered by a dwarf wall and it couldn't have rolled off. I have omitted to mention that we never found out where the pots came from. They certainly weren't ours, because as we collected those that were thrown, we were locking them in the garage with our own.

By this time it was autumn and we had had taps turned on in the kitchen, sounds of small objects being tossed on to the floor, although we only once ever found anything (a tiny metal ferrule of some kind which no one recognised). There was also the episode of the opening dining-room door. We actually saw the handle moving on one occasion. My husband would try to defeat it by rushing into the room from the kitchen, but as soon as we appeared in the dining-room, the door handle would stop moving!

In November the cars began to move (or perhaps it was October). One Sunday afternoon, I looked out of the front door for some reason or other and thought that my car, which had been parked locked in front of the garage, seemed to be much nearer to front door than usual. Then my son came home and said that surely I'd moved my car. I looked out again and the car was in yet a different position, but I thought we'd all made a mistake. Lo and behold, within twenty minutes my car had moved right over to the front door. After this I would park right over by the fence and every night for weeks and weeks my car would be moved as much as nine feet sideways, whilst locked and withe the handbrake on, across gravel, without making a sound. The only indication we had that it had moved, was that it would suddenly appear in front of the sitting room window. There was rarely a mark in the gravel, sometimes a tiny pile up of stones by a tyre. At this time my husband was still pooh-poohing the idea of anything supernatural. The car would often have moved between 5 o'clock and when he came home from work at around 6.00. Up to that time his own car, parked on the other side of the drive, had never been moved.

This particular evening we were going out and we were excitedly discussing the distance my VW had moved in a particularly short period that night and that it must be supernatural. My husband was his usual sceptical self and so my son said to him 'Challenge it then to move your car and see what happens'. 'Right. If there's anything there I defy you to move my car' said my husband sardonically. We all went to the door and his car had been moved across the drive and parked so close to my own that they were almost touching! The 'thing' became so adept at moving my car, that some mornings I could actually drive out forward instead of reversing out onto the main road!

This was still going on together with the flashes and other oddities, and Christmas was about three weeks away when we had the occurrence of the flying ashtray and keys. The two boys were upstairs doing their homework, I was also upstairs washing my hair and my husband was downstairs watching TV. I came down to go into the sitting-room and just as I was closing the door, there was a loud crash. The bunch of keys which I always leave on the telephone table in the hall had been thrown at the sitting-room door just as I was closing it. The boys came down of course to see what the excitement was and having put the keys back on the hall table and closed the door they were thrown again. The next time my husband put them back on the table and trapped them under a small silver ashtray, which contained a bit of old cellotape and an unbroken length of cigarette ash. No sooner had we closed the door than both ashtray and keys hit it, but the amazing thing was the contents of the ashtray were undisturbed – the ash hadn't even disintegrated. These episodes also became frequent occurrences. About three days before Christmas, my mother arriced to stay and the ashtray and keys struck the sitting-room door five times in succession. Needless to say she was terrified and had there been any more trains to London that night she would have returned there.

Also at Christmas we had a strange experience with voices on the telephone. The interferences was still continuing on the line whenever the phenomena were mentioned. Then one evening, my brother rang and I happened to ask during the course of conversation 'Can I bring Mum up to your house on Boxing Day as we're going out in the evening?' During the extremely short gap before he replied, clearly over the line but sounding a long way off, came my voice repeating that sentence exactly. My brother recognised my voice as well. My husband – ever the disbeliever – said it must be the party line playing about. But the next night he had occasion to ring his sister, who asked about the 'thing'. He was telling her about the latest car movements and said 'and the car was moved many feet to the side', then he too heard his own voice in the distance saying that sentence over again, as did his sister. This happened on one other occasion, also to my husband, and it was the only time I have ever seen him pale throughout all the weird things that happened to us!

One of the last things to happen was as follows. In January at about 9 o'clock in the evening, we were watching TV when we saw a brilliant flash through the curtains over the French windows at the back of the house. We had become so blasé by now that we took no notice but the next day when I went out to the garden, I saw that the long teak bench outside the French window had been tipped on its side onto the dwarf wall. I rang my husband at work and told him that the flash had been to draw our attention to its latest antic. I put the bench back and wedged it in between the wall of the house and the terrace wall. That night there was a flash again at 9 o'clock and we drew back the curtains to see if the bench had been tipped up again. We really couldn't believe our eyes, but the bench had gone! My husband and the boys took torches out to the back garden, but it wasn't to be seen anywhere. I must say here that we have a completely enclosed garden and the only way is either through the house, the locked garage or the side door which is permanently locked. There was just no way the bench could have been taken. When they had scoured the back garden, I just happened to stroll across the sitting-room and look out, out of the front window. There jammed in between the bow window and my husband's car was the three-seater bench! It had arrived completely silently and without damaging anything. The only way to get the wretched thing back into the garden, was to unlock the side door which we kept permanently locked. The angles of the doors in the house and garages are such that the bench is too long to manoeuvre round them.

The next night (my son and I having replaced the bench in its accustomed position) there was a flash again around nine o'clock and of course the bench had gone again. but this time it was found under a tree on the far side of the garden!

It was around this time that I telephoned Mr. Macnaghten. Everything happening to us was so amazing, that we simply had to tell someone else about it.

We would all like to say that throughout everything that happened, there was never any sense of evil. In fact whatever it was seemed bent on making us laugh and when we did all laugh out loud, it seemed to be spurred on to doing even more outrageous things. The only person frightened at all was my mother, who is in any case of a very nervous disposition (and even more so now!)

The day Mr. Macnaghten and his wife arrived, the 'thing' had been very busy flashing and switching off all the power points on the wall (some of these are tucked away under shelves and are very inaccessible, and in any case this was a new trick and we thought at first that our TV and record player had both broken). Mr. Macnaghten recited the gist of a prayer or saying that his mother had used in Scotland to get rid of a poltegeist and we have had nothing at all from that day'.